Visitor's
Guide
To

ARIZONA'S
INDIAN
RESERVATIONS

By
Boye De Mente

PHOENIX BOOKS/Publishers
Phoenix, Arizona
USA

Copyright © 1976 by Boye De Mente. All rights reserved.
Published by Phoenix Books/Publishers,
1641 E. McLellan Blvd.,
Phoenix, Arizona 85016 USA.
ISBN 0-914778-14-5

Note from the Author

I am grateful to the many people who helped me in compiling the information for this book—in particular the several tribal officials who read the manuscript when it was in rough draft. But I alone am responsible for any omissions, errors and all opinions in the book—B.D.

CONTENTS

3 MOUNTAIN RESERVATIONS

4 CENTRAL DESERT & RIVER RESERVATIONS

5 SOUTHERN ARIZONA RESERVATIONS

ONE

Indian Country!

A rizona is one of the best-known of the 50 American states, not only among Americans but also among people all over the world. The state owes its fame to several wonderful circumstances, the most important of which are (1) its spectacular desert and mountain scenery; (2) its healthy, invigorating climate; and (3) *its Indians!*

Arizona was *Indian Country* when the first Europeans set foot on the American continent, and it is still *Indian Country* today!

There are well over 150,000 Indian residents in Arizona, representing 17 tribes and living on 23 reservations that encompass a total of over 20,000,000 acres—*or some 27 percent of the total land area of the state!*

Days of the Old Ones!

Indians have lived in Arizona for at least 25,000 years—and probably for more than 30,000 years. Archaeologists have discovered and studied evidence of three major tribal groups whose earliest histories are cloaked in the dust of ages: the *Anasazi,* who lived in the northern plateau highlands of the state; the *Mogollon People,* who lived in the northeastern and eastern mountain belt; and the *Hohokam* who lived in the central desert areas.

These early Arizona Indians, like other North and South American Indians, were related to the peoples of Asia. At first, they were gatherers and hunters, stalking and killing huge elephants (yes, elephants in Arizona!), camels, horses, sloths and bisons.

Among the sites where evidence of these ancient Arizonans has been found is Ventana Cave, about 100 miles west of Tucson on the Papago Indian Reservation; and near Naco, south of Bisbee on the Arizona-Mexico border.

Several thousand years after the first signs of these three groups, or around 7,000 B.C., a group known as the *Cochise People* arrived on the scene. (They are called "Cochise" because they left the most traces of their existence in what is now Cochise County in southeastern Arizona.)

It is believed that the *Anasazi,* the *Hohokam* and the *Cochise People* changed from being primarily hunters to farmers, raising corn and later squash and beans, around the year 2000 B.C.

The *Hohokam,* who flourished in the Phoenix-Scottsdale area until about 1400 A.D., were master canal-builders. The present-day canal system serving Phoenix and the *Valley of the Sun* is an extension of the ancient *Hohokam* network.

There is some evidence to suggest that the *Hohokam* may have migrated into the Phoenix area from central Mexico because of the similarity of their temples and sunken handball courts to those of the *Toltec* and *Mayan* cultures.

The *Hohokam* were a sophisticated and cultured people. They wore finely woven and elaborately decorated clothing. They were master stone sculptors, and used etching techniques not discovered in Europe until 1500 A.D. The *Hohokam* vanished from the Phoenix Valley of the Sun around 1400 A.D., although present-day Pimas who live just south of the Phoenix area are believed by some to be their descendants. *Hohokam* is a Pima word meaning "Those Who Are Gone."

The *Anasazi* (and this is a Navajo word meaning "The Ancient Ones") were scattered over a wide area in northern Arizona. They lived in hundreds of small villages or towns—now called *pueblos*—and built three, four and five-story apartment houses. Some of these houses were out in the open; others were in the mouths of caves and beneath huge overhanging cliffs. Several of these extraordinary dwellings still stand.

The *Anasazi* wore clothing made of cotton, along with sandals and sashes. They enjoyed music. Their towns and apartment complexes were graced by plazas. Their temples (*kivas*), partly sunken into the ground, sometimes measured 70 feet in length.

The civilization of "The Ancient Ones" is believed to have reached its peak between 1000 A.D. and 1300 A.D., with thousands of pueblos dotting the rugged plateaus and mesas of northern Arizona. Then something happened that almost destroyed the world of the *Anasazi.* Some believe that the several inches of topsoil, laid down on the hard-surfaced plateaus centuries before by volcano eruptions, finally blew away, causing a drastic reduction in the population, and scattering most of the survivors to the winds.

There was a brief recovery by the *Anasazi* around 1400 A.D., when a number of even larger towns were built. But by the 1500s only three of these population centers remained: the Hopi in northern Arizona, and the Zuni and Rio Grande people in New Mexico. The Spanish, who arrived on the scene in

1540, counted only 70 villages in northern Arizona in the latter part of the 1500s. Today, there are "about" 26 recognized pueblos remaining.

Archaeologists say the *Mogollon People* were the least advanced of the early Arizona Indians—perhaps because the streams and forests of their mountain homeland provided them with the food they needed, and there was little pressure to develop a higher culture.

The Navajo and Apache, two of Arizona's largest and best-known contemporary tribes, are believed to have arrived in Arizona between 1200 and 1400 A.D., from northern regions. They came as nomadic hunters.*

The Coming of the Conquistadors

In 1520 and 1521, Spaniards, driven by a lust for gold and new lands, captured, looted and enslaved the Aztec Empire of Mexico. For several years thereafter, they kept hearing rumors of seven cities in the far north that were allegedly paved with gold—the fabled *Seven Golden Cities of Cibola* that had been mentioned in earlier Spanish literature!

In 1539, the Viceroy of *New Spain* (Mexico) commissioned Marcos de Niza, a Franciscan monk who had been with Pizarro when the latter pillaged and destroyed the gold-rich Inca Empire in Peru, to travel northward, locate the seven cities and determine the extent of their wealth.

The Apaches

*The origin of the name *Apache* is uncertain. Historians suggest it may have derived from the Zuni word *Apachu,* meaning "People"; or from the Ute word for Apaches, *Awatche.* The first recorded use of the word is in an account written by the Spanish explorer Onate in 1598, who referred to the *Apades* or *Apiches*.

Linguistically related to the Athapaskans of Alaska, Canada and Northern California, the Apaches are believed to have arrived in the Southwest between 1000 and 1500 A.D., settling in southwestern Colorado, New Mexico, western Texas, Arizona and northern Mexico.

When European Americans began arriving in the Southwest there were seven major Apache groups in these areas—the Lipan Apache (now virtually extinct), Jicarilla Apache, Kiowa Apache, Mescalero Apache, Chiricahua Apache, Western Apache and Navajo.

The Western Apaches, which included the present-day White Mountain Apaches, Cibicue Apaches, San Carlos Apaches and Northern and Southern Tonto Apaches, were dominate in east central Arizona. Each of these five sub-tribal groups of the Western Apaches were divided into two to four bands or clans, primarily based on geographic location. These clans were further sub-divided into "local groups," each headed by a chief. At the start of the Arizona Indian Wars, there were some 20 of these Western Apache clans, and several dozen "local groups."

De Niza chose as his scout a huge black man named Esteban, who had earlier walked from Florida across the southern portion of the North American continent to the Gulf of California with his shipwrecked master, Cabeza de Vaca.

When his little band approached what is now the southern boundary of Arizona, De Niza sent Esteban on ahead with some Indian escorts, with instructions for him to send a runner back with a tiny cross if the stories about the golden cities were false.

If the stories were true, however, Esteban was to send back a cross 12 inches high. If the cities were found to be richer than Mexico, he was to send back a "large" cross. When the black man departed from De Niza's camp, he thus became the first non-Indian of record to set foot in what is now Arizona.

Four days after Esteban left the main party, he sent back a cross as large as a man. One can only imagine the glee and enthusiasm with which De Niza set out to follow his scout.

In the meantime, Esteban continued marching northward, passing through numerous Papago and Pima Indian villages. The huge black man was the first non-Indian these people had ever seen, and they treated him with extraordinary awe and respect, showering him with gifts.

As Esteban proceeded from one village to the next, he gradually decked himself out in brilliant clothing and ornaments. Taking on kingly airs, he commandeered a retinue of Indian men to carry his growing horde of gifts, and assembled a harem of pretty Indian girls for his nightly pleasure. His reputation began to precede him.

Here the story becomes a little confused. Arriving at the mesa village of *Hawikuh* in present-day New Mexico, which he believed was the first of the seven golden cities of Cibola, Esteban's diplomacy failed him. He was attacked and killed outright, or was captured, confined for the night, then put to death the next morning.

In any event, some of the Indians accompanying Esteban escaped and hurried back to Fray Marcos with the bad news. It took some doing, but the intrepid monk managed to prevent his own guides and bearers from deserting him by luring them on with gifts and promises.

De Niza and his party pushed on, arriving at the outskirts of *Hawikuh* at dusk, when the mesa village seemed to glitter in the setting sun. This was enough to convince the frayed monk that he had indeed found the fabled golden cities. He returned to Mexico City and reported to the Viceroy that his trip had been successful.

A year later, in 1540, a great expedition of horsemen, foot soldiers, bearers, and drivers herding cattle, sheep, goats and horses—all under the command of Francisco Vasquez de Coronado—set out from Mexico City to conquer and loot the fabled cities of gold, and establish settlements in the new land.

Two years later, Coronado returned to Mexico City without any gold, his decimated army in tatters and hungry, and his own health undermined. Raiders instead of prospectors, Coronado and his men found none of the treasure that lay barely concealed beneath the rock and soil of Arizona. But they had made one of the great exploratory marches in history, going all the way to what is now Kansas before turning back.

The year Coronado arrived in Arizona, its Indian population could be divided into desert/river tribes, mountain tribes, and plateau/canyon tribes, according to the geography of their ancestral lands. The desert/river tribes included the Pima, Maricopa, Papago, Cocopah, Quechan, Mohave and Chemehuevi. The mountain Indians were the Yavapai and Apaches. The Hualapai, Havasupai, Hopi, Paiute and Navajo made up the plateau/canyon tribes.

These tribes were of varying sizes—some little more than nomadic bands. Each had its own language, religion, traditional customs and manners.

The desert/river tribes, mostly farmers, tended to be friendly and helpful to the Spaniards. The more free-spirited and aggressive mountain and plateau Indians were often hostile toward the invaders, however, and lost many warriors in clashes with the mounted and better-armed Spanish.

The Coronado Expedition was followed in subsequent decades by other groups of Spanish explorers, by the inevitable missionaries, and finally by a few settlers.

But the Indians of Arizona were to escape the full force of the blood-lust of the Spaniards because of a simple but vital fact—their disdain for gold; that soft, muddy-yellow metal for which "civilized" people have historically sold their souls!

It was an insatiable lust for gold that had brought these first Europeans into Arizona, but finding that the Indians possessed little of it and discovering only a few minor "strikes" in the territory as the decades rolled by, the Conquistadors were content to leave the original inhabitants of Arizona to the mercy of the missionaries and a limited number of Spanish farmer/ranchers. Both the missionaries and the settlers frequently misused and abused the Indians in their vicinity, but they made no effort to exterminate them.

The Spanish Conquistadors believed that they had taken possession of Arizona "by the will of God." By the same token, the missionaries felt it was their divine mission to destroy the native religions of the Indians, and to change their life-styles to conform with that of Spanish peasant-slaves.

But the missionaries were few and far between. Despite their claims of having 43 churches and 34,000 converts among the Navajo and Hopi by 1627, and the establishment of a number of missions and ranches in southern Arizona, their influence was more economic than religious. During the almost 300 years of the Spanish Period in Arizona (1539–1821), most of Arizona's Indians went about their traditional ways, undisturbed.

The Indians who were put upon by Spanish priests, settlers and soldiers often gave as good as they got, occasionally rising up and completely destroying the missionaries, their missions and the settlers.

From the Spanish, various of the tribes obtained horses, sheep, goats, cattle and many new vegetable crops, and were thus much better prepared for the events that were to take place in succeeding decades. It is therefore possible to say, from this distant perspective, that the Indians of Arizona may have, at least initially, gained more than they lost from the coming of the Conquistadors and priests in the 16th century.

But the next great turn of the wheel of history was not to treat the Indians of Arizona so kindly.

The Mexican Period

In 1819, the dispossessed Indians of Mexico, the new race of mixed-bloods sired by the Spanish overlords but disclaimed by them, and the third, fourth and fifth generations of Mexican-born residents of Spanish descent, rose up in a mighty rebellion against Spain, and in 1821 won independence for Mexico.

As momentous as this was for Mexico proper, it caused nary a ripple in the lives of most Arizona Indians. The Spanish troops stationed at the *presidio* (walled fort) in Tucson were replaced by Mexican troops, and there was a small influx of Mexican settlers into the southern part of the territory. But the Mexican Period in the story of Arizona's Indians was to be little more than a footnote.

The Golden Knell of Death

It was not to be the Mexicans but the Americans who were to bring the seeds of death and destruction to well over half of the Indian population of Arizona—and an end to the world they had known since the dawn of their history.

In the late 1820s, American beaver trappers—the so-called Mountain Men—began appearing on the rivers of northern and central Arizona. Travelers, going to and from the central and eastern states to California, also began to cross the territory of Arizona.

By the 1830s, a tide of Americans had begun to roll across the Great Plains, pouring into Kansas, Oklahoma, Texas, New Mexico, the Dakotas and Rocky Mountain region, precipitating the final confrontation with America's surviving Indian nations. Most of the Indians who had historically lived east of the Mississippi River had already been surrounded, mostly decimated and the subdued survivors moved to the vast reaches of the Western Plains. The Plains Indians watched all this with growing alarm.

The U.S. Government justified its confiscation of Indian lands and the removal of Indian populations by an extraordinary cultural arrogance translated as "the right of discovery"; a policy spelled out in a Supreme Court decision in 1823.

This piece of plastic logic said that discovery of the American continent by Europeans "gave" (them) an exclusive right to extinguish the Indian title of occupancy, either by purchase or by conquest. The decision went on to say that this right took precedence over all other rights, and that the U.S. Government alone could hold title to any and all lands claimed by Indians.

As a final clincher, this same Supreme Court decision said that Indians were to be considered as mere "occupants" of the lands they lived on, and while they were to be "protected" as long as they were peaceful, it was specifically spelled out that they were "incapable of transferring title (of their lands) to others."

Americans of this period seemed possessed by a frenzy for moving ever Westward and putting their mark on this great expanse of land. Clashes with the Plains Indians—the Comanches, Cheyennes, Kiowas, Arapahoes, Sioux, the Pawnee, Blackfeet, Crow, Osage and others—became more frequent and bloodier.

These incidents brought about a mood in the U.S. that was graphically described by President Andrew Jackson in 1833 when he told Congress that all Indians of the West would either have to be driven into remote areas and confined there forever because they could not be allowed to live among Whites . . . or they would have to be "exterminated."

The "American" Conquest of Arizona

During the 1830s and early 1840s, traffic between the eastern and midwestern states and California picked up. Travelers passing through Arizona spread the word about its scenic beauty; its forests, meadows and river valleys; about the warm winter climate and the seductive charm of its central and southern deserts.

The number of Americans in Arizona grew from a few dozen to a few hundred, and included farmers, cattlemen, sheepmen, prospectors and desperadoes. In 1846, war broke out between the U.S. and Mexico, and shortly thereafter American cavalry troops made their first appearance in Arizona.

When the war ended in 1848, Mexico ceded all of California, the northern portion of Arizona and the remaining Western slice of New Mexico to the U.S. This brought a new influx of American farmers and cattlemen into Arizona.

But the event that was to spell doom to most of the remaining Plains Indians and bring the Indians of Arizona on stage in a direct confrontation with the armed might of the United States, was the discovery of gold in California on January 24, 1848. Thereafter, the rush of Americans westward, around and through Arizona, became a stream that was to eventually grow into a tidal wave.

Many of the gold-seekers on their way to California got no further than Arizona. Others stumbled onto attractive oases in the deserts and mountains and decided to stay. The pressure on the Indian tribes of the territory became more and more intense with each passing year. Violent clashes between Indians and Whites became commonplace. More U.S. troops were sent into the territory to protect the settlers and travelers.

In 1854, the U.S. bought the southern portion of Arizona from Mexico (the Gadsden Purchase), bringing the settlements of Tucson and Tubac— then the largest communities in the territory—under American jurisdiction. This brought in yet another wave of Americans who continued to settle on the best farming and ranching lands.

This year marked the date of the beginning of "official" U.S. government interest in the growing conflict between the Indians and white residents of Arizona. By the mid-1850s, American leaders in Tucson and the other tiny communities scattered around the territory were calling for a "permanent" solution to the "Indian problem."

The Ultimate Solution

Arizona's Indians were probably saved from virtual extinction by George W. Manypenny, who was Commissioner of Indian Affairs from 1853 to 1857. Manypenny urged that instead of "removing" or annihilating Arizona Indians, that land be set aside for their exclusive use.

It was not until February 1859, however, that the first Indian reservation in Arizona was established, by an Act of Congress. This was the *Gila River Reservation,* just south of present-day Phoenix, where the Pima and Maricopa Indians were confined.

This first Indian reservation in Arizona was not a precedent. The British Colonial authorities had created what amounted to a reservation for Indians in Virginia as early as 1653. The American Government simply decided to adopt a British pattern of dealing with native peoples whom they had overrun in their global expansion.

The first Europeans to arrive on the east coast of North America treated the Indian tribes who lived there as sovereign nations—which they were. The Indians believed there was enough land for everybody, and willingly signed agreements with the new arrivals, ceding them large tracts of their tribal territory. One of the earliest of these treaties was between William Penn and the Delaware Indians, signed in 1682.

After the 13 colonies gained their independence in 1776, the U. S. Government continued to treat Indian nations as sovereign states on the one hand, and the Indians themselves as unwanted, dangerous trespassers on the other.

The U.S. signed its first treaty with an Indian nation in 1878. The last of a long line of 370 treaties was signed 90 years later, on August 12, 1868, with the Navajos of Arizona.

In most cases, the treaties the American Government signed with the many Indian nations were not kept. The people at large would infringe upon the territorial rights of the Indians. The Government would then legalize the infringement by dispossessing the Indians. This happened to the Delawares 18 times. Finally, only a few hundred of them remained, and they ended their days on the barren plains of Oklahoma.

By the 1850s, some white political leaders began to admit that signing more treaties with the still surviving Indians was impractical. They began to push for a much more drastic and permanent solution. The solution finally decided upon was the reservation concept—a specified area of land where the Indians could be confined and kept, by force if necessary, until they were assimilated into the mainstream of American life.

With the establishment of the Gila River Reservation in 1859, the U.S. Government began to formulate a program that sounded simple enough on paper. The Indians were to be isolated on reservations where they would no longer constitute a danger to the white population, and then their life-styles, religions and languages would be eliminated and replaced by the culture of the Whites.

The traditionally peaceful Pimas, Maricopas, Papagos, Hopis, Cocopahs, Quechans, Havasupais and Kaibab Paiutes accepted the American conquest of Arizona with only a few minor rumbles, and over a period of years were all placed on Reservations.

But the idea of confining all of Arizona's Indian tribes to Reservations was easier thought than done. The Hualapai, the Yavapai, the Navajo and the Apache were a proud, independent and aggressive people who did not recognize the "God given" or "Government given" right of white Americans to usurp their lands, to disrupt and destroy their native beliefs and life-styles.

The members of these tribes looked upon the Whites as the trespassers, and were willing and able to fight to protect their ancestral lands and their freedom to come and go as they pleased. War parties from these tribes began to increase the frequency of their raids against outlying ranches, farms, mining camps and wagon trains.

The Whites in turn formed posses and went after the Indian raiders. The Indians occasionally wiped out small parties of Whites; the Whites would then reciprocate, usually killing a larger number of Indians because it was generally a case of rifles against bows and arrows.

Arizona's Indian Wars

The immediate cause of the outbreak of large-scale warfare between Whites and Indians in Arizona, in January 1861, was one of those absurd incidents that have often brought on great tragedies.

A rancher named John Ward lived not far from Apache Pass in southern Arizona with his common-law wife who had once been a captive of the Apaches and had a son fathered by an Apache warrior. One day in January, Ward got drunk and beat the boy so badly he ran away from home. Still drunk (according to historical accounts), Ward went to the local army post and falsely accused Cochise, chief of the Chiricahua Apaches, of kidnapping his step-son and stealing some of his cattle.

A Lt. George Bascom and 54 soldiers were sent to recover the boy and the cattle. Bascom and his troop marched to Apache Pass, where Cochise lived, and set up camp. The next day, Cochise and several members of his family, including two children and a woman, came into Bascom's camp to visit.

Once Cochise and his group were inside Bascom's tent, it was surrounded by soldiers. Bascom demanded that Cochise return the boy and the cattle. Cochise said he didn't have them. Bascom told him he and his party would be held hostage until the missing boy and cattle were returned.

Cochise slit the side of the tent with a knife, dashed through the ring of surprised soldiers and escaped. One of his men who tried to follow him was caught. The soldiers clubbed and bayoneted him to death. The remaining Apache men, children and women were seized and bound.

That evening Cochise and a band of warriors attacked a wagon train going through Apache Pass, capturing two Americans and eight Mexicans. The Mexicans were tied to the wheels of the wagons and burned. The next day Cochise raided a nearby Butterfield Stagecoach Station, captured another American, then offered to trade three captives for the Apaches Bascom held.

Bascom refused and sent for more troops. When they arrived they brought with them three more Apaches they had captured enroute. Cochise's band killed and mutilated the three prisoners they held, then fled into the Chiricahua Mountains. In retaliation, Bascom had the six male Apaches he held, including some of Cochise's kin, hanged.

Cochise declared all-out war against all Americans in Arizona. Lt. Bascom received a commendation from his superiors.

The American Civil War broke out shortly after this, and most of the U.S. troops stationed in Arizona were temporarily pulled out. For some time thereafter, the Yavapais and Apaches raided almost at will, and most outlying American settlements, including Tubac, were abandoned.

In 1861 a troop of Confederate soldiers were temporarily in command of Tucson, the leading American settlement in Arizona. Then a contingent of

Union forces passing through drove the Southerners out. President Lincoln signed a bill making Arizona a Territory in its own right on February 24, 1863. More cavalry troops were sent in and a total of 18 military forts were established in key locations around the new Territory.

In the early summer of 1863 the famous trapper, scout and "Indian fighter" Kit Carson was commissioned a colonel in the U.S. Army, given a large force, and ordered to invade the homeland of the Navajo Indians in northern Arizona, lay waste to it and *kill all male Navajos capable of bearing arms!*

Over the next two years, Carson came close to fulfilling his orders. He marched to and fro in Navajo Land, systematically destroying their crops, orchards, grain stores, horses, sheep and goats; killing the men and older boys, and taking women and children captive. When Carson and his troops entered *Canyon de Chelly*, the last refuge of the Navajos, and destroyed their few remaining farms and food supplies, the survivors surrendered.

During the last months of the campaign against the Navajos, Carson's zeal for killing apparently flagged, because he began to take adult male prisoners instead of slaughtering them.

The once proud Navajo Nation had been reduced to a few thousand starving prisoners of war, with the flower of their manhood gone. These remnants were herded together and marched several hundred miles to a makeshift internment camp in New Mexico. There they were forced to share the camp with the survivors of the Mescalero Apaches, their traditional enemies, who in the meantime had been captured by other troops.

The war against Arizona's Indians continued sporadically. All of the Chiricahua Apaches except Cochise and his band of warriors, were rounded up and eventually shipped to prisoner-of-war camps in Florida. Later they were moved to Alabama and then to Oklahoma, where their descendents were kept imprisoned until 1913. They were never to return to Arizona.

During these years, the Navajos interned at *Bosque Redondo* in New Mexico were literally dying of starvation because their attempts to raise crops failed. A devastating smallpox epidemic hit the camp in 1865, killing over 2,000 of the inmates.

The situation was so bad that Army troops guarding the camp began to close their eyes, allowing some of the Mescaleros and Navajos to slip out and try to make their way back to their homelands.

Finally, in 1868 in the last treaty the U.S. Government was to sign with an Indian nation, the ancestral homelands of the Navajos was officially designated as a Reservation, and the approximately 16,000 Navajos who remained alive were allowed to officially return home. This was to be the only Arizona Indian Reservation to come into being as the result of a treaty. All others were by acts of Congress or Presidential Orders.

The following year, 1869, the Hualapais surrendered. The Yavapais gave up in 1875, and the Western Apaches in 1881. The final campaigns against these tribes were successful only after the U.S. Army began enlisting pacified Apache warriors, and using them both as scouts and fighters. It was the skills of the Indians themselves that led to their downfall and defeat, not the prowess of the regular American army troops.

In 1871 Indian agent Tom Jeffords helped arrange a peace treaty with Cochise. As part of the peace agreement, the traditional homeland of the Chiricahua Apaches was designated as their Reservation. Cochise thus remained free in his own domain, where he died of natural causes in 1874. In 1876 the government abolished the Reservation, moving the remaining Chiricahuas to the San Carlos Apache Reservation, east of Globe.

With all of the tribes confined to reservations, the only "Indian problem" that remained in Arizona were the few rebel chiefs like Geronimo and other lesser known figures who continued to leave the Reservations and raid isolated settlements and wagon trains. These rebels were gradually contained.

Geronimo surrendered for the last time in 1886, announcing simply that there was little he could say except that he would fight no more. He was shipped to an Indian prison encampment in Florida, where he lived to be 80 years old, dying in 1909.

The Indian wars of Arizona were over.

Decades of Darkness

In 1871 the Congress of the U.S. declared that the surviving Indian tribes would no longer be regarded as separate nations, and that there would be no more treaties with them—an action that formalized what had already become working policy.

This action, following inauguration of the practice of isolating Indians on Reservations, then attempting to de-Indianize them, was the culmination of a process by which the Indians were systematically stripped of all or most of their ancestral lands, their freedom and their personal rights as human beings. It also made them subject to a series of bureaucratic programs that were to bring unimaginable suffering, humiliation and degradation onto Arizona's Indians for a period of nearly 100 years.

Once confined to Reservations, the defeated Hualapai, Yavapai, Navajo and Apache Indians were completely dependent on the Federal Government. Having been engaged in fighting, running and hiding for years, they had no crops in the ground, no stored food, no tools, no supply of clothing, and in the majority of cases, no homes. For the first several years on the Reservations, their dependence on government handouts of food, clothing, medicine and whatever else they needed was virtually absolute—and all doled out through the offices of newly created "Indian agents."

This situation would not have been as tragic as it turned out to be if it had not been for the low character, morals and vindictiveness of many of the Indian agents. To say that some of the agents were unscrupulous men is being very generous. In the worst cases, the agents stole almost everything consigned to the Indians, and sold the goods for their own personal profit.

In 1887 American Indians still had "legal" possession of 139,000,000 acres of land, a total area about four-fifths the size of Texas. In that year, Congress passed a law allowing for Reservation land to be "allotted" to individual Indians as their own private property, which they had to pay taxes on to keep. Any Indian land not so allotted could be sold by the Federal Government as "surplus land."

In the next 47 years, or until this law was revoked in 1934, the Indians lost 90,000,000 acres of land; much of it sold out from under them by the Government as a result of conspiracies between Indian agents and land buyers.

Fortunately for Arizona's Indians, only a relatively small percentage of Arizona Reservation lands were allotted under this system. Where allotment did take place (on the San Xavier portion of the Papago Reservation, on the Salt River, the Gila River, the Colorado River Reservations, and 650,000 acres of the huge Navajo Reservation), the acreage has since been subdivided so many times among succeeding generations that none of the descendants of the original title holders now have enough land to sustain them.

With Arizona's Indians isolated on Reservations, the U.S. Government made an all-out effort to "Americanize" them. They were prohibited from practicing their own religions and social life-styles. White teachers, farmers, carpenters and clergymen were assigned to the different Reservations to instruct the Indians in the American way of life.

Indian children were taken from their homes—by force when their parents objected—and placed in boarding schools where they were subject to punishment for speaking their own language, even when at play.

In 1892, the U.S. Government made it compulsory that all Indian children would be sent to such schools, usually run by missionaries and most of them distant from the children's homes. The missionary societies received $85 for each Indian child they enrolled in one of their schools.

In 1896, the Government issued an order that all male Indians would wear their hair short like urban white men.

In 1900, religious leaders persuaded the president of the U.S. to make it compulsory that all Indians attend Christian religious services. The Presbyterians "got" the Navajos; the Lutherans got the Apaches; and the Catholics got the Pimas and Papagos. This edict was not lifted until 1934.

In 1902 a U.S. Supreme Court decision "recognized" that the Congress of the U.S. had the inherent right to unilaterally break any treaty the government had signed with any American Indian tribe.

In 1924 Congress passed a law making Indians citizens of the United

States—as long as they met the same qualifications applying to other nationalities.

Another 10 years were to pass, however, before the Great White Fathers in Washington were to realize that the Government's efforts to destroy the culture of the Indians and make them over in the image of the white man was a dismal failure and had done more harm than good.

In the *Indian Reorganization Act* of 1934, the land-allotment system was ended; Indians were given the right and limited means to hire legal counsel; compulsory church attendance was banned; the right to practice their own religious and cultural ways was restored to the Indians; an arts and crafts board was established to promote a regeneration of traditional handicrafts; the different tribes were encouraged to set up constitutional-type governments and form corporate business charters; programs were legislated to provide professional and technical training for Indians; and other measures were taken to help Indians help themselves.

All of the Arizona Indian tribes except the Prescott Yavapais and Navajos adopted a constitutional form of government that operates much like a city under a council. But the Indian tribes were so demoralized, uneducated and unskilled by almost 100 years of suppression and mistreatment that it was not until the 1950s and 60s that Indian leaders began to emerge and the tribes began to pull themselves together.

American Indians finally received the right to vote in 1948, and only then if they were literate in English. This language provision was struck down by the Supreme Court in 1970.

The last Arizona Indian Reservation to be created was the Tonto Apache Reservation, near Payson, in 1972.

The fate of Arizona's Indians, linked with the reservation concept since 1859, along with the ineptness, the ignorance and the maliciousness of many of the government bureaucrats and minions appointed as their guardians and teachers, has come full circle.

The smaller tribes on smaller Reservations are gradually being absorbed into the lower rungs of overall American society. Their arts, their religions, their languages and traditional customs and manners are disappearing. But the present-day status and promise of the larger tribes on the larger Reservations is something else.

There is no doubt that Arizona's major Indian tribes owe their survival as a distinct people to their forced confinement on Reservations. The Reservation system did not succeed in destroying their cultures. Instead, the Reservations became a refuge where, despite the handicaps and hardships, the Indians managed to preserve the essence of their beliefs and ways.

By the early 1970s, the larger Arizona Indian tribes had achieved political maturity and had learned how to protect themselves with the white man's second favorite weapon—the law.

Arizona's Indian Lands Today

In 1953 a movement was begun to terminate the "special relationship" between American Indians and the U.S. Government. There are those who feel that Indian Reservations are both an anachronism and a threat. As a result of the movement, Congress severed all special ties with several Indian tribes in Oregon, Utah, California, Wisconsin, Idaho, Alabama and Texas.

There has been no indication that Congress might—or could at this time—dissolve Arizona's 23 Indian Reservations.

Besides the 23 Reservations, there are a number of Yaqui Indian communities in Arizona, including *Pascua Village* southwest of Tucson, *Barrio Libre* in South Tucson, and *Guadalupe,* south of Phoenix, which is shared by Yaqui Indians and Mexican-American residents. These Arizona Yaquis are refugees from northern Mexico who fled their ancestral homelands during the Mexican Revolution, when there was a massive effort to exterminate them.

In addition to the 125,000-plus Arizona Indians who live on Reservations, there are somewhere between 30,000 and 40,000 Indians living off-Reservation: in Scottsdale, Phoenix, Tucson, Tempe, Flagstaff, Ajo, Clarksdale, Grand Canyon Village, Holbrook, Page and Winslow; with small percentages in virtually all communities in the state.

Strictly Indian towns on the various Reservations include Bylas, San Carlos, Tuba City, Window Rock, Ft. Defiance, Sacaton and Sells.

There is a sprinkling of Indians in Arizona who moved here from other states. Among them are Sioux, Fox, Omaha, Cheyenne, Arapahoe, Choctaw, Comanche, Osage, Pawnee and Shawnee.

Arizona Indians may leave their Reservations any time they want and return when it suits them. Some tribes have certain restrictions, however. If a Papago marries a non-Indian, the couple cannot live on the Reservation.

Members of each of the various Arizona Indian tribes have the same legal rights regarding tribal property, no matter where they live. But those who do not live on their own Reservation have little or nothing to say about tribal affairs.

Arizona Indians speak 17 native languages and several dialects, and there are regional variations of languages in the larger tribes. Many Navajo and Papago do not speak English, while larger numbers of these and other tribes speak both their native tongue and English; and some speak Spanish as well—a linguistic accomplishment of enviable proportions.

Arizona's Indian Reservations are not truly "sovereign states," as is sometimes suggested. They are more like semi-independent "principalities" that exist at the pleasure of an adjoining great power. The Reservation lands are held "in trust" by the Federal Government for the tribes—in principle, forever—and the Government acts as "guardian," counselor and sponsor to Indians through the powerful Bureau of Indian Affairs.

One "official" explanation of the status of Indian Reservations goes like this: "Arizona Indian tribal governments exercise inherent and sovereign powers, although this sovereignty is limited by treaties, statutes and agreements made with the United States."

American Indians' rights to self-government have been "recognized" again and again in numerous instances over the decades, and were finally summed up in the *Indian Reorganization Act* of 1934 (also known as the Wheeler-Howard Act).

The Act says in part: "Perhaps the most basic principle of all Indian law, supported by a host of decisions . . . is the principle that those powers which are lawfully vested in an Indian tribe are not, in general, delegated powers granted by express acts of Congress, but rather inherent powers of a limited sovereignty which has never been extinguished.

"Each Indian tribe begins its relationships with Federal Government as a sovereign power, recognized as such in treaty and legislation. The powers of sovereignty have been limited from time to time by special treaties and laws designed to take from the Indian tribes control of matters which, in the judgement of Congress, these tribes could no longer be safely permitted to handle.

"These statutes of Congress, then, must be examined to determine the limitations of tribal sovereignty rather than to determine its source or positive content. What is not expressly limited remains within the domain of tribal sovereignty, and therefore properly falls within the statutory category, 'powers vested in any tribe or tribal council by existing law.' "

The relationship between Arizona Indian Reservations and the state of Arizona has been spelled out in much clearer terms. Arizona has a disclaimer law that reads as follows:

"That the people inhabiting said state do agree and declare that they forever disclaim all right and title to all lands lying within state boundaries owned or held by an Indian or Indian tribe, the right or title to which shall have been acquired through or from the United States or any prior sovereignty and that until the title of such Indian or Indian tribes shall have been extinguished the same shall be and remain subject to the disposition and under the absolute jurisdiction and control of the Congress of the United States"—Arizona Law Review, Vol. 4, 1962. P. 61.

The state of Arizona does not have civil or criminal jurisdiction over Indians living on their Reservations. The state is empowered to assume such jurisdiction *with the consent of the Indians concerned,* but there is little possibility that this might happen anytime soon. Arizona has a Commission of Indian Affairs aimed at providing Indian tribes with a means of communicating directly with the state government.

All Arizona Indians who earn an income are required to pay Federal and Social Security taxes just like all other Americans. If they live off-Reservation and own property, Indians must also pay property taxes. Arizona Indians may live on-Reservation and commute to work "outside."

Indians who want to leave the Reservation and seek work may apply for financial assistance from the Bureau of Indian Affairs. Indians have been able to legally sell and consume alcoholic drinks on-Reservation since 1953, but at this point only the Ft. Apache and Gila River reservations allow it.

It should not surprise anyone that many Indians tend to be cautious in their dealings with Whites. Some Indians regard Whites as destructive and wasteful; heartless in their treatment of their environment, their children and their aged parents; and immoral in their religious pretensions.

At the same time, Arizona Indians are friendly, courteous and hospitable people, despite all the ill-treatment and hardships they have endured. They welcome visitors to their Reservations but at the same time, they expect visitors to also be courteous and to respect their personal privacy and rights, as well as their property.

Renaissance of the Red Man

Summing up, the Indians of Arizona, for nearly 100 years, were on the verge of suffering the same fate as the Mohawks, the Mohicans, the Powhatan, the Seneca, dozens of other tribes, and the buffalo. *But Arizona is still Indian Country!*

As said earlier, Arizona Indians' disdain for gold saved them from the Spaniards. The wild ruggedness of the territory's great mountains, plateaus and canyons in the northern and eastern areas; and the dry, cactus-studded deserts of the central and southern portions, kept American settlers and soldiers out of Arizona until quite late in the Westward movement of the country.

And finally, the deep reservoir of strength and stamina of the Indians, coupled with the widespread use of the Reservation system—despite its nearly fatal flaws—resulted not only in the survival of Arizona's Indians but in providing them with a sanctuary, allowed the larger tribes to preserve much of their culture and eventually make a population comeback.

The Navajo, Hopi, Apache, Papago and Pima-Maricopa Indians have moved from the edge of extinction to the beginning of a renaissance—a renaissance that may well see them join the landed gentry of the state by the end of this century; affluent, able, and respected for their economic and political power.

The populations of the Papago, Apache and Navajo tribes, already large enough to make their cultures viable and dynamic, are growing rapidly. Their Reservations are large enough and rich enough in developed and potential resources to give them a major hand in the future of Arizona.

The larger tribes have retained their languages, their understanding and reverence for their environment, and their harmonious view of man and nature—along with at least a part of their ancestral lands.

The present generation of Indian leaders, and the young generation coming of age, have a new sense of awareness and appreciation for their traditional ways, and a growing feeling of pride in their unique Indian identity.

The aim of the tribal leaders today is to develop the Reservations to the point where the younger generations will not need or want to leave. As they succeed, Arizona's Indians will once again take their place as first citizens of the state.

Most Europeans, Asians and Americans in general are fascinated by American Indians. Arizona's Indians invariably rank among the state's top "tourist attractions."

In this respect it should be obvious to state leaders, representatives of the tourism industry, residents and visitors from out-of-state, that while Arizona Indians welcome visitors—and several tribes are in fact working to develop their Reservations into major recreational and sightseeing areas—they expect visitors to abide by the laws of their land, and to behave as guests who might want to be invited back.

The Reservations are private property. The persons and homes of the Indian residents are private. All should be shown the same courtesy and respect you expect for your own person and property.

The Reservation visitor should keep in mind that he or she is quite literally a guest in a "foreign country," where cultural attitudes, social customs and often the language differ. It is the visitor who is the outsider, the foreigner, the guest—and should conduct him or herself accordingly.

MILES TO THE TRIBAL HEADQUARTERS
OF ARIZONA'S INDIAN RESERVATIONS

Arizona Indian Reservations that offer fishing, camping & hunting opportunities require visitors to obtain tribal licenses & permits. In some cases these permits & licenses are available only at Tribal Headquarters. In most cases Tribal Headquarters are also the center of activity on the Reservations. I have therefore included a mileage chart showing the distance (in rounded figures) from Phoenix, Scottsdale & Tucson to the Reservation capitals—B.D.

Reservation	Tribal Headquarters	Phoenix	Scottsdale	Tucson
Akchin	Maricopa	40 mi.	35 mi.	90 mi.
Camp Verde	Camp Verde	100	110	230
Cocopah	West Reservation	210	222	270
Colorado River	Parker	163	175	285
Fort Apache	Whiteriver	180	170	210
Fort McDowell	Ft. McDowell	30	20	115
Gila River	Sacaton	42	30	80
Havasupai	Supai	261	273	390
Hopi	New Oraibi	260	270	320
Hualapai	Peach Springs	205	215	335
Kaibab-Paiute	Pipe Springs	350	360	470
Navajo	Window Rock	310	300	345
Papago	Sells (via Tucson)	190	180	70
Salt River	Salt River	15	5	115
San Xavier	San Xavier Mission	140	130	10
San Carlos Apache	San Carlos	110	100	126
Tonto-Apache	Tonto Village	94	84	185
Yavapai	Prescott	96	108	215

TWO

Plateau & Canyon Reservations

THE NAVAJO NATION

Established in 1868 for the estimated 16,000 Navajos who survived the military campaign against them and the rigors of four years of confinement in a bleak New Mexico prison encampment, the *Navajo Indian Reservation* encompasses some 16 million acres, making it the largest Indian Reservation in the country. Of this total, 1,503,963 acres consist of spectacular canyons and mesas, and another 472,716 acres is covered by commercial timber.

The huge Reservation, which takes up most of the northeastern portion of Arizona and extends on into New Mexico and Utah, is divided into five agencies, each with its own Bureau of Indian Affairs administrative head-quarters—at Ft. Defiance, Chinle, Tuba City, Shiprock and Crown Point in New Mexico, and the Navajo area office at Window Rock. Navajo Tribal Headquarters is also located at Window Rock. The Reservation is governed by an elected body made up of a chairman, vice-chairman and 74 delegates.

Besides possessing the largest Reservation in the country, the Navajos are the most populous of all American Indians, with the total expected to pass 150,000 before long. More than half of the Navajo population is under the age of 20. And with the romantic bent the younger Navajos seem to have, the population is likely to grow at an even faster pace in the future. A common sight on the Reservation is that of young couples in pick-up trucks, sitting so close together either one could be driving!

Land of the Navajo

Navajo Land is a visual experience that makes a lasting impression on the sensitive visitor. The landscape includes some of the most spectacular

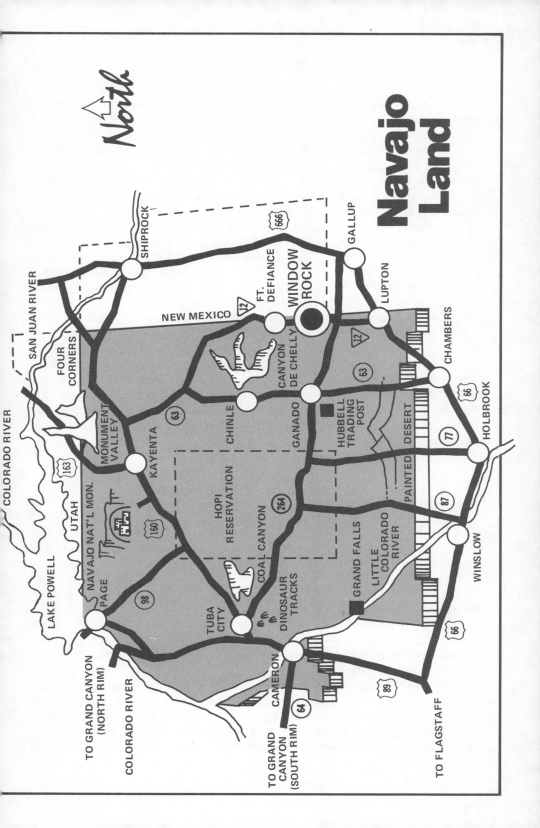

scenery in the world—vast treeless wastes, sagebrush-covered "deserts," multi-colored sandstone mesas and canyons, towering buttes, and massive mountains with their higher elevations cloaked in evergreen trees.

The most distinctive quality of the Navajo landscape is its immensity. It seems to go on forever, and makes one really appreciate the book about Monument Valley called *Land of Room Enough and Time Enough*. Some of the great canyons on the Reservation are 2,000 feet in depth. Some buttes, rising abruptly from flat basin floors, are 2,000 feet in height.

Elevation in Navajo Land varies from 4,500 feet in the desert country, deeper canyons and river valleys, to 10,388 feet at the summit of Navajo Mountain on the Arizona-Utah border. Within this range, there are three major zones—areas that are above 7,000 feet and account for eight percent of the reservation; areas between 5,500 and 7,000 feet and comprising 37 percent of the total area; and the "low zone," which varies from 4,500 to 5,500 feet in altitude and accounts for the remaining 55 percent of Navajo Land.

Mountains traditionally have played a vital role in Navajo life. They have long regarded the higher and more spectacular peaks in their homeland as sacred. Two that are on the reservation or near it are Navajo Mountain, on the Arizona-Utah border, and the San Francisco Peaks, adjacent to Flagstaff just a short distance from the southwestern corner of Navajo Land. According to Navajo beliefs, sacred spirits dwell in these high places, and medicine men make frequent pilgrimages there to pray, pay homage to the spirits and gather herbs for ceremonies and rituals.

Weather in Navajo Land

The climate in Navajo Land is typical of that of the southwest desert and mountain country. Eighty percent of the time, including most of the fall, winter and spring, the skies are a burnished blue, and the sun a golden prominence in the deep, vaulted sky. Frequent high winds blow up sand-storms in the late spring. Summer is the "rainy season" with brief, heavy downpours common from July through September, and often causing flash-flooding in some areas.

Temperatures and precipitation are influenced primarily by elevation. Summers in the high country are warm during the day and cool at night. Winters in the higher elevations are marked by daytime temperatures that may drop to or below zero.

The lower the altitude, the higher the minimum and maximum ranges. Summertime temperatures in the deep canyons and desert areas may soar to over 100 degrees in the heat of the day, and drop to the 70s at night. The main thing to keep in mind is that if you visit the Reservation from late fall to early spring, be prepared for cool to cold days and frigid nights no matter where you are. In July, August and early September in the lower regions be prepared for high mid-day and afternoon temperatures.

Precipitation in the lower desert areas of the Navajo Reservation averages from 7 to 11 inches a year, and almost all of this is in the form of rain. These areas include much of the southern, western and northwestern portions of the Reservation, plus the northern ends of Chinle and Chaco Valleys.

The higher plateaus and lower mesas have 12 to 16 inches of precipitation a year, with about one-quarter of this in the form of snow. The higher mesas and mountain country—the Chuska-Carrizo ranges, Navajo Mountain, the higher portions of the Ft. Defiance Plateau and Black Mountain, and the northern and eastern escarpments—get from 16 to 27 inches of precipitation per year, with almost half of it as snow.

The flora of Navajo Land is also determined by elevation. As the altitude and precipitation go up, the flora changes from sagebrush to juniper, oak, pinon, ponderosa pine, silver spruce, fir and aspen.

The Navajo People

The Navajo people are classified as belonging to the same linguistic group as the Apaches; a group that apparently first flowered in the vicinity of Lake Athapascan in northwestern Canada. But there is no particular Navajo racial type, just as there is no specific Apache type. Like their white counterparts, the Navajo come in many sizes and shapes. But unlike most white Americans, the Navajo tend to be quiet and reserved until they get to know you. Thereafter, they are more open, friendly—and hospitable—than most.

Visitors on the Navajo Reservation should keep in mind that their curiosity about the Navajo and their way of life does not justify an invasion of their privacy or imposing upon them. Navajos welcome visitors, and more often than not go out of their way to help them, but they are a proud people whose beliefs and ways deserve as much respect as the next person's.

There are several specific rules of etiquette to keep in mind while you are on the Reservation. Never take a close-up photograph or sketch a Navajo without his or her permission. If you do photograph or draw a Navajo on any occasion other than a public event where specific individuals are staging some kind of show or exhibition, you are expected to pay a small gratuity because the person or persons concerned are, in effect, working as professional models. The Navajo do not mind having their *hogans* photographed.

Under normal circumstances no one should ever enter a Navajo *hogan* or house without first being invited and guided. It is also improper to camp near a Navajo dwelling or in the immediate vicinity of a private spring, well or pond. (Alcoholic beverages are not permitted on the Navajo Reservation.)

Unless you are solicited, it is very bad manners to attempt to buy jewelry being worn by private individuals. The typical Navajo does not wear jewelry as an advertisement, but as personal adornments or as an indication of his or her wealth. Individual Navajos do, however, sell rugs at numerous roadside locations around the Reservation.

The Navajo engage in a wide range of modern industrial activity, along with cattle and sheep-raising and farming. Large numbers of Navajo also work in the traditional crafts of rug and jewelry-making.

Where the Navajo Live

The Navajo live in over two dozen towns and communities spread around the huge Reservation, and on farms and ranches that are often great distances from each other. Their homes range from the attractive ranch-style houses that are so popular in Phoenix and other Arizona cities, to the traditional *hogans*, which often adjoin conventional "American" styled homes.

The picturesque *hogans* are, of course, most common in the countryside. All of them face the first light of dawn. Older ones are built of logs, mud and earth as in the old days, but there are also some "modern" styled ones constructed of board, with wooden roofs instead of dirt coverings.

Larger communities in Navajo Land are Window Rock, the Tribal Headquarters; Chinle, Ft. Defiance, Ganado, Kayenta, Tuba City and Monument Valley.

Window Rock, which has a population approaching 3,000, takes its English name from the presence of a great hole in a huge, red sandstone formation framing the thriving town. Long before the coming of the white man, both this great hole and a spring below it played a major role in the Navajo *Water-Way Ceremony*.

Situated on the east side of Black Creek Valley among trees and huge mounds of sandstone boulders, Window Rock was the site of an important Indian community as far back as 1300 A.D. Ruins in the area include a multi-room apartment complex just below the great hole in the massive rock overlooking the town.

The growth of Window Rock is visible even to passers-by. New housing and new businesses are going up regularly. Visitor facilities in the busy Reservation crossroads include a large modern motel, restaurants and service stations. Visitor information is available in Window Rock from the Navajo Parks and Recreation Department, tel. 871-4941, ext. 448, 449, 450; or from the Ranger Section, tel. 871-4516.

A good starting place for visitors to Window Rock is the Visitor's Center and Navajo Tribal Museum, located inside the Fairgrounds complex, just south of Highway 264, about a mile west of the center of town.

Ft. Defiance, called *Tse Hoot Soi* or "Meadow On the Rocks" by the Navajo, was also a popular Indian meeting place before the coming of the white man. Its natural springs served as shrines for the Navajo, and the area was an important herb-gathering place for medicine men.

Six miles northwest of Window Rock, Ft. Defiance was headquarters for Kit Carson and his troops when they campaigned against the Navajo in the Indian Wars of the early 1860s. Today the small picturesque community is an important tribal town, with a number of agency offices.

A multi-million dollar sawmill complex is located 15 miles north of Ft. Defiance, adjoining Red Lake Reservoir and near the Ft. Defiance Plateau just to the west, which includes a 600,000-acre ponderosa pine forest.

A geographic novelty known as Black Rock two miles south of Ft. Defiance is actually a long volcanic "dyke," referred to in the Navajo *Wind-Way Ceremony* as Big Snake's House, for a giant snake reputed to live inside the rock.

Ganado, at the junction of Highways 63 and 264, some 48 miles north of U.S. 66 and 30 miles west of Window Rock, has a population approaching 2,000, and is an important trading and handicraft center. The settlement was originally called *Pueblo Colorado,* but the name was changed to Ganado in honor of Ganado Mucho, a head-man of the Western Navajos until his death in 1892—and signator of the 1868 treaty between the Navajos and the U.S. Government.

Ganado is a gateway for Chinle and Canyon de Chelly National Monument, and the site of one of Arizona's most famous Indian trading posts— Hubbell Trading Post. Founded in 1873 by Don Lorenzo Hubbell, the post is still in operation today, and has been designated as a National Historic Site. The National Park Service operates a museum at the Hubbell homesite, and conducts tours through the famous old territorial home. In earlier years, guests at the Hubbell home included a president, dignitaries from abroad, famous writers and artists.

The Hubbell Trading Post and home are a short distance west of the mid-town area. Ganado Lake, to the northeast, attracts local and visiting fishermen. There are numerous archaeological sites in the area.

Chinle, some 40 miles north of Ganado, is "headquarters" for the Canyon de Chelly National Monument. Known as "Running Out" to the Indians —because of the stream running out of the canyon—Chinle also has been an Indian crossroads and settlement for centuries.

Justin's Thunderbird Lodge is the largest and best-known motel in Chinle. Its facilities include a cafeteria, a gift shop, and a service that operates half-day and full-day jeep tours of Canyon de Chelly. If you plan on staying at Thunderbird Lodge, make reservations as early as possible. Mailing address: Box 548, Chinle, Arizona 86503. Tel. (602) 674-5443.

Tuba City, at the juncture of *Navajo Trail* (Highway 160) and Route 68, is the largest and most important community in western Navajo Land. Called

"Zig-Zagging Waters" by the Hopi, Tuba City was once in the domain of the Hopi, and is named after Tuba, a famous Hopi chief.

Eons ago, the land around Tuba City was a garden of lush greenery, and was the home of dinosaurs. Millions of years after the dinosaurs disappeared, horses, camels and elephants appeared and had their day.

Numerous springs—that have survived since the Pleistocene era—first attracted Indians; then in the 17th century the Spanish, and finally in 1875 the Mormons. The Mormons remained for only 28 years. Because of friction with the Navajo over land and water rights, they sold their buildings and improvements to the U.S. Indian Service in 1903 and moved away.

Tuba City is now a thriving agricultural community, and headquarters for numerous Navajo tribal services. It is an important stop-over for visitors heading northeast toward Monument Valley and east toward Hopi Land and the eastern portion of the Navajo Nation. A motel and two restaurants are available.

Kayenta, on a creek 76 miles northeast of Tuba City, is the principal Arizona gateway to Monument Valley. Large pools of water in the vicinity also made this remote spot an Indian oasis for centuries. The community now has traveler facilities and agencies offering conducted tours of Monument Valley.

The Treasures of Navajo Land

In a twist of fate that provides the Navajo with a measure of ironic justice, the plateaus, canyons and mountains to which they were confined back in 1868—then isolated and considered virtually worthless by white America— have since turned out to be a treasure trove of natural resources. The largest privately-owned stand of ponderosa pine in the U.S. is on the Navajo Reservation. Navajo Land also has natural gas and oil wells, coal and uranium mines.

The greatest natural resource of all, however, could turn out to be the potential for the tourist industry. Besides the people themselves, who—again —are living treasures, the Reservation incorporates some of the most spectacular sightseeing attractions in the American Southwest. These include:

Canyon de Chelly National Monument—This rather odd name is a corruption of the Navajo word *Tsegi,* which means "Rock Canyon." In the heartland of Navajo country, this national monument consists of three great gorges, with a combined length of about 100 miles, cut 1,000 feet deep in a huge sandstone plateau. Each of the great canyons is distinguished by massive stone monoliths that tower up to 800 feet above the floors.

Long a dwelling place for Indians, the canyon branches contain many remarkable prehistoric ruins, including the famous *White House* and *Ante-*

lope House ruins. During the Indian Wars, this awe-inspiring geographic wonder was the last refuge of the Navajos, and was invaded by Kit Carson and his army. Carson and others of the time believed erroneously that is was a "fortress" that would be difficult to capture. All they found in the canyon were women, children, the few surviving male Navajos, mostly aged, and completely unprotected farms and orchards.

The stream flowing through the depths of Canyon de Chelly is once again the life-line of small Navajo communities of hogans, corrals, vegetable patches, corn fields and orchards; its inhabitants living much as they did before the coming of the white man.

Canyon de Chelly is 42 miles north of Ganado, and is accessible from the west via Tuba City and Hopi Land; from the south via Holbrook, from the east via Gallup and Window Rock, and from the north via Mexican Water. It is strictly forbidden—and the regulation is enforced—for visitors to go into Canyon de Chelly without a licensed guide—with the exception of a self-guided tour along a well-marked 1.25-mile foot trail to the famous *White House Ruin.*

The National Park Service provides escorts for short walking tours into the outer reaches of the canyon, beginning at 8 a.m. every morning, and covering about three-and-a-half miles. For more extensive sightseeing in the canyon, visitors are required to go in on horseback or by special vehicle. Thunderbird Ranch Lodge operates car tours into the canyon.

The *Visitor's Center* at Canyon de Chelly National Monument head-quarters, on Highway 7 a short distance from Chinle, is open daily the year around, from 8 a.m. to 5 p.m. There is a craft shop and a small museum at the Center, and in the summer months several Navajo weavers operate their looms in the patio. You are expected to pay a small fee to take a picture of the weavers.

There are public drives along the north and south rims of Canyon de Chelly and the west rim of Canyon Del Muerto that have several lookout points offering spectacular bird's eye views of a number of its major attractions.

Visitors who camp their way around Navajo Land will appreciate Canyon de Chelly's *Cottonwood Campground.* Operated by the National Park Service, it has tables, barbecue fireplaces and toilets with running water. Every good-weather evening from May through September Park Rangers present a slide show and lecture about Canyon de Chelly at the campgrounds. The campsite is open all year.

Four-Corners—The only place in the U.S. where four states—Arizona, New Mexico, Utah and Colorado—come together at one point, *Four Corners* is one of the most popular highway stop-overs in the country. A low, granite monument marks the spot. Many visitors like to get down on all fours and have themselves photographed in all four states at the same time.

Grand Falls—On the Little Colorado River east of Highway 89 between Flagstaff and Cameron, these falls can be described as "grand" only after heavy rains further up and during the peak snow run-off periods on the headwaters of the junior Colorado. When the river is high, the water cascades over 185 feet of terraces, throwing up a muddy spray that is indeed spectacular.

Hubbell Trading Post—Mentioned earlier, this is Arizona's best-known Indian trading post, and was designated as a National Historic Site in 1967. The adjoining Hubbell home depicts a history of the Southwest through rare books, Indian crafts and paintings. It is open to the public daily from 8 a.m. to 5 p.m. in winter months, and from 8 a.m. to 6 p.m. (or later) during the summer. The trading post and home are one mile west of Ganado just off of Highway 264.

Monument Valley—In the northern portion of Navajo Land, and extending into Utah, Monument Valley is one of the most extraordinary geographic sights on earth . . . great rolling sand dunes, towering sandstone buttes, arches and spires; in colors that spellbind the mind's eye, as far as the eyes can see. Many major movies, including such classics as *Stagecoach, She Wore A Yellow Ribbon, Clementine, Captain Buffalo* and *The Searchers,* were made here.

A Navajo tribal park, Monument Valley abounds with ancient ruins. Many Navajo residents of the Valley live in the traditional hogans, near tiny oasis-like "swamps." Highway 163 passes along the western edge of Monument Valley, but the most spectacular vistas are off the road, and accessible only by guided jeep-tours from Monument Valley Inn or a Navajo-owned tour by George-Holiday. See Monument Valley Navajo Tribal Park.

The Monument Valley *Visitor's Center,* just off of Highway 163, has a gift shop, and there are campsites and picnic grounds nearby. Commercial tours starting at the Center are advisable for visits to more remote areas of the great expanse, such as Mystery Valley and Cane Valley.

Navajo National Monument—Just west of *Navajo Trail* (Highway 160) between Kayenta and Tuba City, the Navajo National Monument is made up of three of the largest and best preserved cliff-dwelling ruins in the U.S. The first of the monuments, *Betatakin,* which means "Ledge House," is nine miles north of Highway 160 (the turn-off is 50 miles north of Tuba City at Black Mesa Trading Post) via paved road (#564), which deadends at monument headquarters and a Visitor's Center. Betatakin is 1¼ miles from the Visitor's Center via a well-maintained walk-way (roundtrip: 2½ miles).

Betatakin ruins are in a great bowl that forms an almost perfect arch. Dozens of apartments are clustered within the walls of the cliff overlooking Betatakin Canyon. Visitors to the area often appreciate the canyon as much or more than the ruins. It is lush with trees, ferns and reeds, and is a sanctuary for wild-life.

The second ruin, *Keet Seel,* is the largest such ruin in the U.S., and is eight miles to the west of monument headquarters. Visitors may hike to the ruin on their own, or take a guided horseback tour that leaves the Visitor's Center every morning at 8:30 a.m. Arrangements for horses must be made at least a day in advance by contacting monument headquarters at 672-2366.

The third section of the National Monument, *Inscription House,* is some 30 miles from monument headquarters, and is not open to the public at this time. A trading post called Inscription House, about three miles from the ruins, is frequently confused with the monument by visitors seeing highway signs in the area. The trading post is open for business, but Inscription House ruins are closed.

Special Note: Betatakin and Keet Seel are primarily summertime attractions, because the area is 7,000 feet above sea-level and is frequently snowed in during winter months.

A campground near the Visitor Center is open from May 15 through October 15. ·

Dinosaur Land—When you are on the Navajo Reservation you can have the extraordinary experience of standing where dinosaurs once stood, walked, ate, fought and died. Tracks of these great reptiles, including the mighty Brontosaurus, have been found on Hoskinini Mesa, off Route 18 between Monument Valley and Kayenta, and along Route 3 about three miles east of Tuba City. In the latter area were also found fossils of ancient horses, camels and elephants.

Coal Canyon—Surely one of the most unusual sights in Navajo Land is Coal Canyon on Black Mesa, some 14 miles east of Tuba City, toward Hopi Land. The canyon of coal, about a mile off the highway to the north, is a natural "open-pit" mine that the Navajo and Hopi have been mining for generations. There is a small campground on the rim of the canyon.

The above "attractions" are only some of the highlights to be found on the Navajo Reservation. Literally hundreds of square miles of the Navajo Nation are wonderlands of scenic beauty. Some vistas are so compelling they become hypnotic—the kind of scenes one can stare at forever and never become bored.

The Reservation is large. Distances between communities and special landmarks are measured in dozens of miles. To get the most out of your trip to or through the Navajo Nation, slow down, stop often, and savor those in-between miles.

Keep in mind, however, that it is illegal for a Navajo or anyone else to excavate, destroy, have, own or sell any object on the Navajo Reservation that has historic, archaeological, paleontological or scientific value—without written permission from the Navajo tribe and the Secretary of the appropriate

U.S. Government department. This includes picking up pieces of petrified wood or prehistoric pottery, and removing cacti or other living plants.

There are numerous trading posts and arts and crafts shops on the Reservation where you can buy beautiful and valuable Indian-made handicrafts. The *Navajo Arts and Crafts Guild* has shops in several locations, including Cameron, Chinle, Betatakin, Kayenta, Monument Valley Tribal Park headquarters, Teec nos Pos and Window Rock. It is best to do your shopping for Navajo artifacts at these licensed outlets.

Navajo Ceremonial Dances

Ceremonial rituals remain an essential part of Navajo life. Their purpose is manyfold—to keep the people in harmony with nature and the spirit world and to repair and maintain mental and physical well-being. Ceremonies also function as social events in a general sense, bringing people together, often from isolated areas of the Reservation.

Visitors to Navajo Land should keep in mind that the ceremonials are private religious-healing rituals and that they are as much a form of worship to the Navajo as prayer in a church is to a Catholic. It thus behooves spectators to conduct themselves in a circumspect manner, just as they would be expected to do if they were guests at a Christian service—that is, if they are lucky enough to happen onto a Navajo ceremonial dance in the first place.

Tribal fairs and other major annual occasions usually include ceremonial dancing, but these are events that occur only a few times a year at most. The regularly occuring ceremonials are private affairs, arranged and paid for by a family for a member who needs help. The "sings" are thus not announced in advance or promoted as public spectacles. Visitors are permitted to view the ceremonies . . . but they have to find them first. The only way to do this is to make inquiries in local areas, asking the residents if they know of any planned dances.

Ceremonial dances are usually held late at night, beginning around midnight, outside the home of the patient, and are marked by large bonfires frequently visible from nearby highways. If you are driving through inhabited areas of the Reservation at night and spot a fire off the highway, chances are it is a "sing." If you can find an access road and make your way to the site, you will be permitted to watch.

Navajo dances are based on myths and legends. The three most popular are the *Enemy-Way Dance* (sometimes called "The Squaw Dance"), the *Yeibichai Ceremony* or Night-Way Dance, and the *Fire* or *Corral Dance*.

The Enemy-Way Dance is a summer, mind-healing and purifying ceremony, frequently performed to help people suffering from nightmares and other frightening illusions. The "sing" lasts for three nights, with the activity in a different place each night. The name "Enemy-Way" apparently refers to doing away with the enemies of one's mind and body. Calling the ceremony a

"Squaw Dance" derives from the custom of Indian girls of latching onto male spectators and dragging them into the dance circle, then charging their willing or unwilling partners a small fee for each round they dance. Most men accept this bit of playful extortion with good humor. When the ceremony ends at dawn, the participants roast a freshly slaughtered sheep for breakfast.

The Yeibichai Ceremony, usually performed during the winter months, is intended to aid individuals suffering from nervousness or insanity, and lasts for a period of nine days. The eighth night is "initiation night," when young boys and girls are told the secrets of the rituals. The ninth and last night of the ceremony is considered the most impressive by those who have seen it.

The Corral or Fire Dance seeks divine help in warding off potentially fatal snake-bites and lightning. It is named from the fact that part of the ceremony takes place within a "corral" of branches surrounding a bonfire.

If you are going to look for a "sing," be sure to take a powerful flashlight with you—for walking dark roads, finding your car, etc.

Spectator Events

There are several annual events on the Navajo Reservation that attract visitors from all over the Southwest. The major ones:

July Celebration—Held on the 3rd weekend in July, this 3-day event includes a rodeo, ceremonial dances, a parade with marching bands, and other activities—at Window Rock.

Navajo Tribal Fair—This colorful event, the largest Indian fair in the world, is held each year over the 1st weekend in September, at the Fairgrounds in Window Rock. It is the largest and most important annual event on the Reservation, and includes a rodeo, horse racing, evening ceremonial dances, weaving and silversmithing, handicraft booths, food stalls, produce and livestock exhibits, contests of various kinds and a Miss Navajo pageant in which "Queens" from the five agencies compete for the Miss Navajo title.

Northern Navajo Fair—The largest celebration in the northern portion of the huge Navajo Reservation, this event takes place in Shiprock (New Mexico) on the 1st weekend in October. It includes a rodeo and all the usual Indian fair trappings.

Western Navajo Fair—Held on the 2nd (or 3rd) weekend in October in Tuba City, this is Western Navajo Land's equivalent of the larger tribal fair at Window Rock.

Tribal Parks in Navajo Land

Navajo Land has several tribal parks, ranging from a few acres in size to well over two million acres, that encompass some of the most stunning natural scenery on earth, and have a variety of visitor facilities.

Kinlichee Tribal Park—This 640-acre park, near Cross Canyon Trading Post on Highway 264, 22 miles west of Window Rock and eight miles east of

Ganado, includes a complex of ruins that date back to the Anasazi culture.

The park has a self-guiding trail that takes the visitor past all the ruins and a number of wayside exhibits. There is a small picnic grounds on a hillside overlooking the ruins and some nearby Navajo fields. The park begins 2½ miles from Cross Canyon Trading Post, via a dirt road.

Lake Powell Navajo Park—Adjoining the southeastern shore of Lake Powell, and comprising 2,218,112 acres of northwestern Navajo Land, this great park is mostly wilderness area, noted for ruggedness, scenic beauty and archaeological sites. Within its boundaries are two national monuments: Rainbow Bridge National Monument, and Navajo National Monument.

The park includes some 400 miles of Lake Powell shoreline (out of a total of 1,800 miles!). There are visitor facilities at the two national monument headquarters, and at Page and Wahweap.

Little Colorado River Gorge Navajo Park—In the far west portion of Navajo Land, this 360,992-acre park extends to the eastern boundary of Grand Canyon National Park.

The park sets astride the canyon of the Little Colorado River where the latter joins the Colorado in the upper reaches of the Grand Canyon. The park is wild, rugged and spectacular. There is a Visitor's Center and a Navajo Arts & Crafts Guild shop at the junction of Highways 64 and 89 (just south of Cameron), and an off-road viewpoint where Highway 64 parallels one of the most scenic points along the gorge, further on. Stop in at the Visitor's Center for local details.

Monument Valley National Park—Covering 30,000 acres and lying astride the Arizona and Utah border in northwestern Navajo Land, this park encompasses *Monument Valley,* often called "The Eighth Wonder of the World."

The starting point for visits to Monument Valley is the park headquarters and Visitor's Center, reached by a 4-mile access road from U.S. 163, which begins at Kayenta and bisects the Valley.

Navajo Tribal Rangers at the park headquarters provide visitors with detailed information about the park, and collect a small entrance fee. From the Visitor's Center, sightseers may take a 16-mile loop drive that winds around the Valley. Commercial tours into the more rugged areas of the park are also available at the Center.

The Visitor's Center includes an Arts & Crafts Room, and area exhibits. A campgrounds and picnic area is adjacent to the Center.

Window Rock & Tse Bonito Navajo Parks—These two small parks (121 acres) are on the outskirts of Window Rock; *Tse Bonito* to the south and *Window Rock Park* to the north and east. Tse Bonito takes in several large sandstone monoliths known as "The Haystacks" (and was the first stopping place when Kit Carson and his troops herded the defeated Navajo from Ft. Defiance to New Mexico in 1864).

Only limited camping facilities are available at Tse Bonito. Window Rock

Park north of town has camping and picnic grounds, with water and restrooms.

Fishing & Hunting on Navajo Land

There are more than 20 lakes and reservoirs, providing over 5,000 surface acres of fishing waters, on the Navajo Reservation—plus several mountain streams in the Chuska Mountain Range. The fishing season for residents and visitors alike is year-around. There is no limit on such common species as bullheads and sucker, but trout, channel catfish and bass are limited to eight each per day.

Only hook-and-line fishing is permitted on the Reservation, but fishermen have a wide choice of bait that may be used—worms, water-dogs, insects, marshmallows, cheese, corn, salmon eggs, fire-balls and prepared catfish bait.

Youngsters up to 14 do not have to have permits if they are with a licensed adult, but their bag-limit is half of the adult limit.

Permits are on sale at the Navajo Fish and Wildlife Office in Window Rock; at Fed Mart in Window Rock; the Canyon de Chelly Trading Post, and Fleming D. Begaye & Company in Chinle; the Kayenta Trading Post in Kayenta; the Tuba City Community Center; and Hutch's Sporting Goods in Winslow.

Among Navajo Reservation fishing lakes in Arizona are Many Farms Reservoir, one mile east of the town of Many Farms on Highway 8; Ganado Lake, just east of the town of Ganado on Highway 264; and Pasture Canyon Reservoir, about five miles east of Tuba City. Cold-water fishing lakes on the reservation include Fluted Rock, Tsaile, and Wheatfields; all in the Chuska and Lukachukai Mountains in northeastern Navajo Land. Warm-water lakes stocked with bass, crappie and blue-gill include Many Farms, Ganado, Red Lake and Round Rock Lake.

All established fishing lakes on Navajo Land have campgrounds and toilets. Best idea if you plan on fishing during your visit to the Reservation is to write to the Fish and Wildlife Department, P.O. Box 339, Window Rock, Arizona 86515, and ask for a detailed brochure on the subject.

The Navajo do not promote hunting on the Reservation by non-Indians because game animals are not plentiful.

Camping Parks on Navajo Land

There are several tribal parks in Navajo Land where visitors are invited to camp. Among the most convenient: Monument Valley Tribal Park, a few hundred yards beyond the monument headquarters, which is four miles north of Highway 160; the Window Rock Tribal Park, just below the famous landmark rock; and Tse Bonito Park, south of Window Rock. The KOA Campground near Goulding's Lodge in Monument Valley is also popular.

REST AREAS & CAMPING FACILITIES IN NAVAJO LAND

Name	Location	State	Route No.	Facility	Drinking Water*	Tables	Fire Places	Ramadas	Pit Privy
Aneth	2 mi. E. Montezuma Creek	UT	Hy 262	Picnicking	None	5	5	5	4
Antelope Lake	9 mi. N. Pine Springs	AZ	Country Rd	Fishing	None	2	2	0	1
Asaayi Lake	11 mi. E. Navajo	NM	Country Rd	Fishing	Camp	0	0	0	0
Beautiful Valley	11 mi. SW Chinle	AZ	Route 8	Rest Area	None	2	2	2	2
Berland Lake	13 mi. N. Crystal	NM	Country Rd	Fishing	None	0	3	0	0
Black Mesa	Jct.—Nav. Nat'l Mon. Hy 64	AZ	Hy 64	Rest Area	Station	3	3	3	2
Bowman Mem. Park	3 mi. S. Oak Springs	AZ	Country Rd	Picnicking	None	10	10	0	4
Buffalo Pass	8 mi. E. Lukachukai	AZ	Country Rd	Picnicking	None	2	2	0	2
Camel Butte	Monument Valley Park	AZ	Country Rd	Picnicking	Station	1	1	0	0
Cameron	Arts & Crafts	AZ	Hy 89	Rest Area	A & C	2	2	2	0
Cpt. Tom Reservoir	4 mi. N. Newcomb	NM	Off Hy 666	Fishing	None	0	0	0	0
Cliff Dwelling	2 mi. NW St. Michaels	AZ	Country Rd	Picnicking	None	2	2	0	0
Coal Mine Mesa	N. Coal Mine M. Rodeo Grd.	AZ	Country Rd	Picnicking	Windmill	2	2	0	0
Cross Canyon	1 mi. E. Cross Canyon T.P.	AZ	Hy 264	Rest Area	T.P.	1	1	1	0
Cutter Dam	8 mi. S. Blanco	NM	Off Rt. 17	Picnicking	None	10	0	0	0
Deer Springs	Country	AZ	Blue Canyon	Picnicking	Springs	2	2	0	0
Dennehotso	2 mi. E. Dennehotoso T.P.	AZ	Hy 64	Rest Area	None	2	2	0	0
Dinosaur Tracks	5 mi. W. Tuba City	AZ	Hy 64	Rest Area	None	2	2	2	2
El Captain Butte	9 mi. N. Kayenta	AZ	Hy 464	Rest Area	None	1	1	1	0
Elephant Feet	1 mi. E. Red Lake T.P.	AZ	Hy 164	Rest Area	None	3	3	3	2
Fluted Rock Lake	5 mi. Old Sawmil	AZ	Country Rd	Fishing	None	2	2	0	0
Fort Defiance	1 mi. N. Ft. Defiance	AZ	Sawmill Rd	Picnicking	None	4	4	0	1
4-Corners Monument	@ Monument	AZ,UT,CO,NM	-	Picnicking	None	10	10	10	10
Ganado Lake	1½ mi. E. Ganado	AZ	Off Hy	Fishing	Mission	3	2	0	0
Grand Falls	16 mi. N. Luepp Comp. Sta.	AZ	Off Hy 15	Picnicking	None	5	4	5	2

*T.P. = Trading Post

Name	Location	State	Route No.	Facility	Drinking Water*	Tables	Fire Places	Ramadas	Pit Privy
Gray Mountain	Reservation Line	AZ	Hy 64	Rest Area	None	1	0	1	0
Hidden Lake	15 mi. S. Summit	AZ	Country Rd	Fishing	None	0	0	0	1
Howell Mesa	26 mi. E. Tuba City	AZ	Hy 264	Rest Area	None	1	1	1	1
Hunters Point	1 mi. E. Hunters Point Sch.	AZ	Country Rd	Rest Area	School	3	2	0	0
Jeddito Jct.	Jct. 264 Route 6	AZ	Hy 264	Rest Area	None	2	2	2	1
Kayenta	3 mi. W. Kayenta	AZ	Hy 64	Rest Area	None	2	2	2	2
Kinlichee Park	2½ mi. N. Cross Canyon T.P.	AZ	Off Hy	Park	None	3	3	3	2
Kit Carson Cave	3 mi. N. Church Rock	NM	Off Hy	Scenic	None	0	0	0	0
Little Colorado	Lower Overlook	AZ	Hy 64	Scenic	None	3	2	2	0
River Gorge	Upper Overlook	AZ	Hy 64	Scenic	None	4	4	4	0
Many Farms Lake	1 mi. S. Many Farms T.P.	AZ	Off Hy	Fishing	None	0	0	0	0
Mariano Lake	1/2 mi. Mariano Lake Sch.	NM	Off Hy	Fishing	School	0	0	0	0
Mariano Pass	6 mi. NE Mariano Lake Sch.	NM	Country Rd	Rest Area	None	2	1	0	0
Marsh Pass	2 mi. E. Nav. Nat'l Mon. Jt	AZ	Hy 64	Rest Area	None	2	0	0	2
Mexican Water	Jct. 12 & 64	AZ	Hy 64	Rest Area	None	1	1	1	0
Middle Mesa	5 mi. W. Red Lake T.P.	AZ	Hy 64	Rest Area	None	2	2	2	2
Monument Valley	Monument Valley Station	AZ	–	Camping	Station	16	16	16	8
Morgan Lake	4-Corners Power Plant	NM	Country Rd	Fishing	None	5	5	8	3
Nazlina Overlook	3 mi. S. Nazlini School	AZ	Country	Picnicking	None	2	2	2	0
North Rain God Mesa	Monument Valley Park	AZ	Valley	Picnicking	None	1	1	0	0
North Window	Monument Valley Park	AZ	Valley	Picnicking	None	1	1	0	0
Owl Springs	6 mi. E. Crystal	NM	Hy 32	Picnicking	Springs	2	2	0	0
Painted Desert View	8 mi. W. Tuba City	AZ	Hy 64	Rest Area	None	1	1	1	1
Pasture Canyon	1 mi. E. Tuba City	AZ	Off Hy	Fishing	None	3	3	0	0
Pinon Jct.	Jct. Route 4	AZ	Route 8	Rest Area	None	2	2	2	2
Red Lake	N. Navajo	NM	Route 12	Fishing	T.P.	0	0	0	0
Red Mesa	Red Mesa T.P.	AZ	Hy 164	Rest Area	T.P.	2	2	0	0
Red Rock Jct.	6 mi. SW Shiprock	NM	Hy 666	Rest Area	None	2	2	0	0

*T.P. = Trading Post

43

Name	Location	State	Route No.	Facility	Drinking Water*	Tables	Fire Places	Ramadas	Pit Privy
Red Wash	3 mi. E. Beclabit	NM	Hy 164	Rest Area	None	1	1	1	0
Round Rock	Round Rock Lake	AZ	Route 12	Picnicking	None	3	3	3	1
Round Top	4 mi. W. Ganado	AZ	Hy 264	Rest Area	None	3	2	1	1
Sage Lake	10 mi. NE Navajo	NM	Off Hy	Fishing	None	0	0	0	0
Scout Pond	3 mi. SW Navajo	NM	Off Hy	Fishing	None	2	2	0	1
Shiprock	Shiprock Com. Park	NM	Hy 666	Campground	T.P.	7	7	0	2
Snake Springs	6 mi. NE Burnside Sta.	AZ	Route 8	Rest Area	None	2	2	2	0
South Rain God Mesa	Monument Valley Park	AZ	Valley	Picnicking	None	1	1	0	0
Squirrel Springs	11 mi. E. Navajo	NM	Country	Picnicking	Windmill	5	3	0	1
Summit (St. Mich.)	8 mi. W. Window Rock	AZ	Hy 264	Campground	None	15	13	0	5
Tuba City Summit	9 mi. SE Tuba City	AZ	Hy 264	Rest Area	None	1	1	1	1
Todacheene Lake	1 mi. N. Washington Pass	NM	Country	Fishing	None	0	0	0	0
Tsaile Lake N. Shore	1/2 mi. S. NCC Campus	AZ	Off Hy	Fishing	College	2	2	0	2
Tsaile Lake S. Shore	2 mi. Off Route 12	AZ	Off Hy	Fishing	College	2	2	0	2
Tse Bonito Park	NM & AZ State Line	AZ	Hy 264	Picnicking	None	2	2	2	3
Wagon Wheel	8 mi. E. Lukachukai	AZ	Country	Picnicking	None	6	5	0	2
Washington Pass	5 mi. E. Crystal	NM	Country	Picnicking	None	1	1	0	1
W. Mexican Springs	5 mi. W. Mexican Springs	AZ	Country	Picknicking	None	2	1	0	2
Window Rock	Headquarters	AZ	-	Picknicking	Com. Sta.	12	6	0	2
Wheatfields Lake	44 mi. NE of Window Rock	AZ	Route 12	Camping	None	26	23	0	13

*T.P. = Trading Post

Overnight Facilities
In Navajo Land

Chinle

Canyon de Chelly Motel, Chinle, Arizona 86503. Tel. (602) 674-5288.

Thunderbird Lodge, Chinle, Arizona 86503. Tel. (602) 674-5443 or 674-5265. Cafeteria; tours of Canyon de Chelly.

Kayenta

Holiday Inn, Monument Valley, Kayenta, Arizona 86033. Tel. (602) 697-3221. Restaurant, arts and crafts shop, swimming pools. At intersection of Highways 160 & 163.

Sands Tours & Cafe/Trailer Park, Kayenta, Arizona 86033. Tel. (602) 697-3550. Weekly and monthly rates; tours arranged.

Tsegi Canyon Motel/Trailer Park, Kayenta, Arizona 86033. Tel. (602) 697-3432. Eleven miles west of Kayenta. Trading post, grocery store. Rates by day, week or month.

Wetherill Inn, Kayenta, Arizona 86033. Tel. (602) 697-3231. Restaurant nearby; tours arranged.

Tuba City

Van's Trading Post/Motel, Tuba City, Arizona 86045. Tel. (602) 283-5343.

Window Rock

Window Rock Motor Inn, Window Rock, Arizona 86515. Tel. (602) 871-4108. Restaurant, coffee shop, banquet facilities, meeting rooms, daily luncheon buffet from 11:30 a.m. to 1:30 p.m.

Window Rock Lodge Restaurant, Window Rock, Arizona 86515. Tel. (602) 871-4466.

MILEAGE CHARTS FOR THE NAVAJO NATION & HOPI LAND

Going North/South on U.S. 89

N. Flagstaff City Limit	10.1 miles	Sunset Crater Turn-Off
Sunset Crater Turn-Off	14.4 miles	Wuptaki Nat'l Monument T-O
Wuptaki Nat'l Monument T-O	20.4 miles	Junction State Road 64 to South Rim Grand Canyon
Junction S.R. 64	1.5 miles	Cameron
Cameron	0.12 miles	Little Colorado River
Little Colorado River	13.9 miles	Junction U.S. 160
Junction U.S. 160	42.8 miles	Junction S.R. 89A
Junction S.R. 89A	25.1 miles	Page/Colorado River

Going Northeast/Southwest on U.S. 160

Junction 160/89	10.5 miles	Tuba City
Tuba City	22.0 miles	Red Lake Trading Post
Red Lake Trading Post	1.3 miles	Elephant Feet Campgrounds
Elephant Feet Campgrounds	29.2 miles	Navajo Nat'l Monument T-O
Navajo Nat'l Monument T-O	20.5 miles	Kayenta Post Office
Kayenta Post Office	41.0 miles	Mexican Water Trading Post
Mexican Water Trading Post	35.3 miles	Four Corners (state line)

Going North/South on U.S. 163

Kayenta Post Office	23.2 miles	Arizona-Utah border/Gouldings Lodge, T.P.

Abbreviations: S.R. = State Route; T.P. = Trading Post; T-O = Turn-Off

46

Going East/West on Route 264
Through Hopi Land

Tuba City	45.0 miles	Hotevilla, 3rd Mesa
Hotevilla, 3rd Mesa	3.5 miles	Old Oribi, 3rd Mesa
Old Oribi, 3rd Mesa	3.0 miles	New Oribi, foot of 3rd Mesa
New Oribi, foot of 3rd Mesa	7.5 miles	Shongopovi, 2nd Mesa
Shongopovi, 2nd Mesa	2.5 miles	2nd Mesa Post Office
2nd Mesa Post Office	8.0 miles	Polacca, foot of 1st Mesa
Polacca, foot of 1st Mesa	11.5 miles	Keams Canyon Trading Post
Keams Canyon Trading Post	43.0 miles	Ganado Trading Post
Ganado Trading Post	30.0 miles	Window Rock, Navajo Capital
Window Rock	153 miles	Tuba City

Going North/South on Route 87

Winslow, on U.S. 66	70 miles	Second Mesa, Hopi Land

Going North/South on Route 77

Holbrook, on U.S. 66	65 miles	Keams Canyon, Hopi Land

Going North/South on Route 63

Chambers, on U.S. 66	39 miles	Ganado, Navajo Land
Ganado, Navajo Land	38 miles	Chinle, Turn-Off for Canyon de Chelly
Chinle, Canyon de Chelly T-O	29 miles	Round Rock Trading Post
Round Rock Trading Post	32 miles	Mexican Water Trading Post

Going North/South on Route 12

Lupton, on U.S. 66	25 miles	Window Rock, Navajo Capital

Abbreviations: S.R. = State Route; T.P. = Trading Post; T-O = Turn-Off

47

HOPI LAND

The *Hopi Indian Reservation,* established on December 16, 1882, is unique in that it is completely surrounded by another Reservation—the much larger Navajo Nation. Total area of Hopi Land is 2,472,254 acres, but at this writing only 650,000 of this acreage is exclusively controlled by the Hopi. The remainder is classified as *Joint-Use Land,* and is "shared" with the Navajos. The Hopi have maintained for years that the Navajo have monopolized and over-grazed the joint-use land, and are seeking to gain exclusive rights to it.

Hopi Land extends from the eerily beautiful *Painted Desert* on the south, to high pine and piñyon country on the north. Within this immense swatch of land are deserts of multi-colored sand, great sand dunes, gulches, washes, canyons, highrise buttes, mesas, grasslands and forests of juniper and pine. Well over half of the land is made up of treeless, windswept valleys and plains broken in many places by spectacular mesas and equally spectacular canyons.

The Hopi People

The Hopi people trace their history in Arizona back more than 2,000 years, and their history as a people back many thousands of years. Their legends tell of a Great Flood and other events that mark them as one of the oldest living cultures on earth. The Hopi legends also tell them that their ancestors wandered for centuries in search of a place where the vibrations were good, and crops would grow. Some claim that the high mesas where they finally settled in northern Arizona is the vibrational center of the planet.

The Hopi are direct descendants of the ancient Anasazi, who occupied the land between San Francisco Peaks near Flagstaff and Canyon de Chelly in what is now Navajo Land. Clan and tribal traditions say they began to gather in the area where they now live during the 1200s.

One of the Hopi villages, Old Oraibi, has been inhabited since this early period, and is regarded as the oldest continuously inhabited settlement in the United States. It is not the oldest Hopi village, however; having been populated by people from Shungopavy village, which used to be located below the present site.

The Hopi did not war against the Spaniards or the Americans, but contact with white men nearly destroyed them anyway. Hopi records say that in 1643 their population numbered some 14,000. That year, small-pox, brought in by white men, killed over 11,000 of them. By 1775 the population was back up to 10,846. Between 1780 and 1781, small-pox struck again, leaving fewer than 900 Hopi alive. Seventy-five years later—in 1853/54, when their numbers

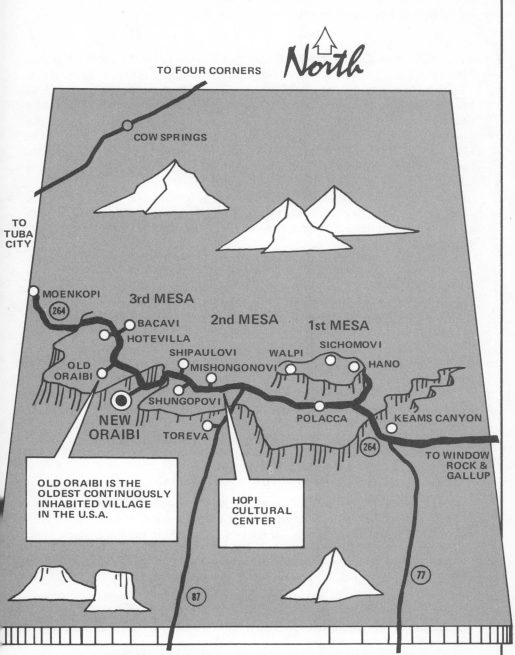

TO FOUR CORNERS

North

COW SPRINGS

TO TUBA CITY

MOENKOPI

264

3rd MESA

BACAVI

HOTEVILLA

2nd MESA

1st MESA

SHIPAULOVI

WALPI

SICHOMOVI

OLD ORAIBI

MISHONGONOVI

HANO

SHUNGOPOVI

NEW ORAIBI

TOREVA

POLACCA

KEAMS CANYON

264

TO WINDOW ROCK & GALLUP

OLD ORAIBI IS THE OLDEST CONTINUOUSLY INHABITED VILLAGE IN THE U.S.A.

HOPI CULTURAL CENTER

87

77

TO WINSLOW & U.S. 66

TO HOLBROOK & U.S. 66

Hopi Land

were back up to 8,000—the Hopi were again ravaged by the deadly disease. That time only 2,000 survived. Today there are approximately 7,000 Hopi.

The Hopi people are divided into clans. They are a deeply religious people who long ago came to terms with their physical environment and their relationship with the spiritual world. Their religion not only teaches peace and goodwill; they live it. A few Hopi are "listed" as having been converted to Christianity, but as in the case of most conversions of people with ancient, highly refined cultures, "it should be noted that any estimate regarding Christianization of the Hopi is questionable."

Long famous for their pottery, baskets, Kachina dolls and jewelry, the Hopi also practice a fascinating kind of "dry farming"; raise cattle, sheep, goats, horses, mules and burros; and engage in various other kinds of private enterprise.

All of the Hopi livestock except sires are individually owned. On numerous tiny "dry farms" (one-quarter to four acres in size) at the feet of mesas and on the slopes of gulches and small canyons, they raise corn, beans, squash, melons and other crops. The Hopi do not plow their deserty fields— which may not look like fields at all to outsiders. They simply poke deep holes in the ground with sharpened sticks, and drop the seeds in. Most farmers have several small fields in different locations because the rainfall that does occur is usually in localized showers, and some fields may receive none at all during the growing season.

The Hopi are governed by a Tribal Council in accordance with the tribal constitution and its bylaws. Nine of the 12 villages on the reservation are represented on the Council, whose office is at New Oraibi. Each village is also organized independently, with an hereditary chief or an elected governor.

Where the Hopi Live

Most Hopi live in the 12 villages on the Reservation, and most of these villages are on the top of or at the foot of three famous mesas—First Mesa, Second Mesa and Third Mesa—which project out from the huge Black Mesa to the north like thick fingers.

Most of the homes on the three highrise mesas are built of stone and logs, and are hundreds of years old. Those at the foot of the mesas are generally much younger, and include many that are built of modern materials in contemporary designs. A few Hopi families live on outlying farms and ranches. Ownership of all Hopi property is passed down through the maternal side of the family.

Arizona Highway 264 (Navajo Route 3) disects the Hopi Reservation on an east-west axis, skirting or passing over each of the three Hopi mesas. Where the highway skirts the feet of the mesas, side-roads lead to the high, elevated villages—part of which are visible from the highway below.

Going from east to west on Highway 264, Keams Canyon is the first community on the Hopi Reservation—but it is *not* a Hopi village. The attractive little settlement is an agency and government town. The Hopi Indian Agency headquarters is there, and all but a few of the town's buildings are owned by the government. The only commercially or privately owned facilities in the town are two trading posts and their adjoining structures.

Keams Canyon, eight miles long and several hundred yards wide at its widest, is a scenic oasis in the desert, however, and is an interesting place to stop over briefly. *Inscription Rock,* so-called because Kit Carson chiseled his name into it, is about two miles up the canyon from the community. There are picnic areas along the canyon road going to the well-known rock.

First Mesa is 15 miles west of Keams Canyon. The village at the foot of the mesa is called Polacca. There are three villages on top of the mesa— Hano, Sichomovi and Walpi. Walpi is the most spectacular of the Hopi villages. Terraced into a narrow rock table, with cliff-edge houses and breath-taking views, it appears unchanged for centuries. This village is also especially known for its ceremonial dances, while the other two villages are rated higher for their pottery and Kachina dolls.

Walpi is undergoing restoration to preserve the natural scenic beauty of the village, and to make it safer for the residents to live and perform their religious ceremonies.

Second Mesa is 10 miles west of First Mesa. The mesa-top villages here are Shungopovy, Shipaulovi and Mishongonovi. The tiny settlement at the foot of Second Mesa is Toreva. It is inhabited by Christianized Hopis, and is not a recognized Hopi village. On Third Mesa, a short distance further west, are the villages of Bacavi, Hotevilla and Old Oribi. New Oribi is at the foot of Third Mesa, a few hundred yards off of the highway to the left, just before it climbs to the top of the mesa. Hopi Tribal Headquarters are located in New Oribi.

The Third Mesa villages are also known for their ceremonial dances, and for their twined basketry, Kachina dolls and sashes.

The village of Moenkopi, some 45 miles west of Hotevilla, near Tuba City, is regarded as a typical Hopi village. It sets in a small canyon, with stone-adobe houses, orchards and tiny farms in the flatter areas and among the sand dunes. (Near the village are the footprints of dinosaurs, embedded in rock!)

The highway passes near Old Oraibi atop Third Mesa, reputedly the oldest community in the country, but as of this writing it is closed to outside white visitors because of the behavior of visitors in the past (digging up graves, stealing sacred ceremonial articles, etc.). The other Third Mesa villages—Hotevilla and Bacavi—have also been the target of "raids" by tourists, and therefore tend to be wary of visitors.

The Hopi are a reserved and private people, but they are naturally hospitable, and are genuinely friendly toward those who show them courtesy and respect—when they get to know them. The best time to visit any of the villages is during dance ceremonies, because then they are expecting visitors.

The Weather

A high, desert area on the Colorado Plateau, with elevations varying from 5,000 to 6,500 feet, Hopi Land gets only about 10 inches of rain a year. About one-third of this falls as showers in July and August. It usually snows throughout most of the Reservation several times each winter, but the snows are light and soon gone from everywhere except shaded areas.

The scarcity of clouds and moisture in the air results in wide temperature changes between day and night, as is typical of the Southwest deserts. Midsummer temperatures are usually in the 90s, and there are days when they pass 100. At night it drops into the 70s and 60s. In mid-winter, the average daytime highs range from the 30s to the 70s; frequently falling as low as zero at night. In the spring and fall, the weather is usually delightful—warm to cool days, and cool to cold nights. There is quite a bit of wind during the early spring months; summers also tend to be breezy. Because of the overall terrain and dryness, there are no year-around rivers or mountain streams on Hopi Land. Water is obtained from springs, wells, temporary surface tanks and earthen reservoirs.

Tourism and the Hopi

The Hopi tribe did not begin to develop tourism as an industry until the 1970s. Prior to this, there were thousands of visitors to the Reservation each year, but most of them passed on through with only brief stops, or stayed only a few hours to view a ceremonial dance and do a little shopping.

The primary reason for this late start in the tourist industry was the reluctance on the part of many Hopi elders and conservatives to expose their unique culture to the unsettling influences of the outside world. The Hopi are still conservative in their acceptance of tourism as a business, and visitors are asked to respect their feelings. (Nowadays it takes a pretty arrogant and narrow-minded individual to claim that the white man's way is the best, and to advocate forcing it on somebody else!)

Because of this feeling among the Hopi, tribal authorities have drawn up a set of rules which visitors are asked to follow. The rules are:

1) Visitors are welcome, but while on the Reservation they should remember that they are guests of the Hopi, and act accordingly.

2) The introduction of intoxicants, or any article whatsoever which produces alcoholic intoxication, on the Reservation is prohibited by law.

3) The molestation of shrines, or removal thereof of such articles as prayer sticks or sacred stones, is prohibited by Federal law. All Hopi ruins are also protected by this law.

4) Photographing, recording and/or sketching of villages, religious ceremonies or individuals is strictly prohibited on the Reservation, unless permission is granted by the village chief or governor.

5) Before spending any length of time in any village, permission should be obtained from the village leader (nearly all Hopi speak English). With the exception of Indian agency employees, non-Indians may not reside on the Reservation without the consent of the respective village head.

6) The maximum speed limit on the Reservation is 55 miles per hour. Drivers are cautioned to watch for livestock on the roads and highways, especially at night.

The Famous Hopi Ceremonial Dances

Each Hopi village has a plaza where ceremonial dances are held today much as they have been for centuries. Most of the ceremonies last for several days, but the major portions are conducted in the underground *kivas,* where only the initiated may witness them. The parts that outside visitors are permitted to watch usually occur on weekends.

Each of the tribal clans has its own rituals—some of them secret. Individuals in these groups are charged with the responsibility of performing the ceremonial dances properly for the benefit of all. Many of the dances are supplications for rain; most also seek to maintain and improve the tribe's harmony with nature, thereby enhancing the prospects of its members for good health and a long, happy life.

The exact starting times of the various Hopi religious ceremonies are determined by the elders according to the position of the sun, the moon, and the physical and spiritual vibrations of all the elements. The schedules therefore cannot be set in advance to the minute or the hour, and both participants and spectators must simply wait until this attunement is achieved.

But the ceremonial dances that outsiders are permitted to observe almost always start at or near sunrise, on Saturdays or Sundays. They then continue intermittently through the day, with breaks for lunch, rest periods and secret rituals conducted in the underground kiva chambers. The ceremonials usually end at dusk. Several of the villages often hold dances on the same day, giving visitors an opportunity to witness parts of several dances by spending a few hours each in different villages.

Among the Hopi dances held in the spring and summer are the so-called "Social Dances" and Kachina Dances, the Snake Dance, and the Flute Ceremony.

Two of the most colorful and interesting of the Social Dances are the Butterfly Dance and the Buffalo Dance. The Kachina Dances are perhaps the most popular of the Hopi Dances. In these, the dancers wear masks and costumes representing various Kachinas, who are messengers of the gods. The dancers are believed to actually become the spirits they represent during the ceremonies.

The Powamu Ceremony or Bean Dance is basically a fertility ritual, held in late February, aimed at enhancing the summer harvest. The ceremony covers a span of several days, beginning in the kiva where beans are sprouted, then continuing out in the open. The Powamu Ceremony takes place in the early spring, and is regarded as the first important Kachina ceremony of the season.

The most publicized of the Hopi ceremonials is the Snake Dance, usually held in the third week in August. This is primarily a rain dance, for which the Hopi believe it is necessary to communicate with the Underworld through live snakes, which live in the ground. Snakes used in the ceremony include deadly sidewinder rattlers. Many visiting spectators look upon the Snake Dance as a kind of side-show. To the Hopi it is a serious and sacred business.

Spectators are allowed to watch only the last day of the Flute Ceremony, during which members of the clan are initiated into the Gray or Blue Flute Societies. On the final day, the ceremony tells in symbolic language how the Hopi came into this world, and the story of their centuries of wandering before they found their present place.

Again, it is strictly forbidden to photograph or sketch the ceremonies, or to make tape recordings. Spectators are expected to watch in silence and in no way interfere with the dancers who must follow elaborate, precise patterns for the dances to be correct and effective.

Since the mid-day sun is usually very bright on the high plateaus, and in July and August can get very hot as well, many visitors bring parasols. Some also bring lightweight folding chairs to sit on while watching the lengthy dances.

When *Are* the Dances?

The Hopis are reluctant to pin down exact dates for any of their dances. The Bean Dance is usually in late February. The Snake Dance is usually on the 3rd weekend in August. There are Kachina dances in at least one village every weekend from May through July. Social dances occur on weekends in mid-summer. The so-called "women's dances" occur on weekends in the latter part of September and early October.

The museum at the Hopi Cultural Center on Second Mesa includes a mural that indicates the approximate dates on which the traditional Hopi dance ceremonials are staged.

Other Visitor Attractions

The principal visitor attractions on the Hopi Reservation are the mesa villages themselves, along with the colorful and intriguing dance ceremonies that climax their various religious festivals. There are also the handicrafts for which the Hopi have long been famous. For these artifacts, as well as a historical perspective of the Hopi culture, one of the best places to visit is the *Hopi Cultural Center,* adjacent to the highway on Second Mesa.

This attractive tourist complex, built in part-pueblo style, includes a motel and restaurant, a museum and three craft shops—Dawa's Jewelry, Hopicrafts, and the Silvercrafts Cooperative Guild. The three craft shops are both owned and operated by Hopi. The motel and cafe are owned by the Hopi tribe, and leased out to Hopi businessmen for operation.

Other places where visitors may buy Hopi craftwork: at the Hopi Silvercraft Cooperative Factory just west of the Cultural Center; at Hopi Enterprises in Oraibi; Second Mesa Trading Post; Paul Saufkie Trading Post on Second Mesa; Oraibi Trading Post in Oraibi; Pollacca Trading Post in Pollacca; and the Keams Canyon Trading Post.

Visitors may also buy Hopi craftwork from individual craftsmen and women in the villages. Pottery is available in First Mesa villages, coiled baskets and plaques at Second Mesa, and wicker baskets and plaques at Third Mesa. Kachina dolls and silvercrafts are found in all of the villages.

Overnight Facilities on Hopi Land

Besides the 33-unit motel and restaurant at the Hopi Cultural Center on Second Mesa, there is also a 24-unit motel with cafe in Keams Canyon. Reservations are important if you plan on putting up at either of these two places.

For reservations and other details about the Cultural Center motel, call the Hopi Cultural Center at (602) 734-2401, or write P.O. Box 67, Second Mesa, Arizona 86043. For the Keams Canyon Motel, call (602) 738-2297 or write Keams Canyon Motel, Keams Canyon, Arizona 86034.

Nearby off-reservation accommodations are available in Tuba City, Cameron, Window Rock, Holbrook and Winslow. For those who wish to camp out in Hopi Land, there are overnight camping facilities next to the Cultural Center on Second Mesa, with water, power and sewer hook-ups for some 40 units. A small Hopi Tribal Campground at Keams Canyon, across from the Keams Canyon Trading Post, has toilets, trash cans and water available; but no utility connections as of this writing. A small overnight fee is charged.

There are also small campsites on Second Mesa, between the Hopi Cultural Center and the nearby Silvercraft Cooperative Factory, and east and west of New Oraibi, but no services or water are available. There is no charge at these latter sites.

Medical Note

Visitors may obtain emergency treatment at the U.S. Public Health Service Indian Hospital in Keams Canyon—but the cases must really be emergencies. The nearest regular public medical services are at Ganado, on the Navajo Reservation; and in Holbrook, Winslow and Flagstaff.

Other Tourist Notes

There are no tourist offices or chambers of commerce on the Hopi Reservation. Public phones are available at Keams Canyon, and at one or more locations on each of the three Mesas (but as of this writing, not all of the villages have bothered with telephones.).

HUALAPAI LAND

Established on January 4, 1883, the *Hualapai Indian Reservation* is almost a million acres large—993,173 acres to be exact. The reservation boundary on the north is formed by the Colorado River, which it shares with Grand Canyon National Park. The eastern boundary adjoins Grand Canyon Park and the enlarged (1975) Havasupai Indian Reservation.

Westward, the Hualapai Reservation extends to Music Mountains and Grand Wash Cliffs. Private ranches and Federal land form most of the southern boundary. A short strip of U.S. Highway 66 (Interstate 17) passes through the southern tip of the reservation. Peach Springs, where Tribal Headquarters are located, is on Route 66 in this section—some 50 miles northeast of Kingman.

The topography of the Hualapai Reservation (sometimes incorrectly spelled "Walapai") varies from desert plateaus, ponderosa pine-forested hills, chaparral-filled valleys, grasslands, and rugged canyons that stair-step their way down to the depths of the Grand Canyon. Elevation on the Reservation ranges from about 1,200 to 7,400 feet. Hualapai Land includes most of the mountainous areas of Arizona's Mohave County, and portions of Yavapai and Coconino Counties.

The Hualapai People

The Hualapai belong to the Yuman language stock of Western Indians, which includes—among others—the Yavapai, Havasupai and Mohave Indi-

South

TO FLAGSTAFF

TO KINGMAN

PEACH SPRINGS

66

PEACH SPRINGS WASH →

DIAMOND CREEK

QUARTERMASTER
VIEW POINT

COLORADO RIVER & GRAND CANYON

GRAND CANYON NAT'L PARK

MEAD NAT'L RECREATION AREA

Hualapai Res.

ans. The Hualapais were friendly toward the first white Americans who visited and settled in their part of Arizona, and often helped them. But after a number of their leaders were killed, the Hualapais took up arms against the Whites.

Eventually the Hualapais were defeated by U.S. Army troops, and the survivors were herded into a camp near Parker, on the Colorado River, where many more of them died. Those who survived this ordeal defied agency orders and marched back to their homeland. Finally, agency authorities decided to allow the Hualapais to occupy a small part of their traditional lands. A few years later this area became the present Reservation.

Today the Hualapai, who number about 1200, are cattlemen, construction workers, craftsmen, Government employees, and retail traders. Peach Springs, the only town on the Reservation, has a population of about 900.

The Weather

Hualapai Land has mostly clear, warm-to-hot days and cool nights in the summer, with thunderstorms common in July and August. It is mostly bright and clear in the winter, but snowy periods are common. Daytime temperatures in winter range from around freezing to 60° F. At night, temperatures can drop to zero in unprotected areas.

Visitor Attractions

Tourism is an important and growing industry to the Hualapai. Each year thousands of visitors pass through the Reservation on U.S. 66, stopping over in Peach Springs for services, to shop at the Hualapai Arts and Crafts Center, and to visit the Tribal Cultural Center.

The Reservation offers visitors hunting, fishing, hiking and camping opportunities, plus the opportunity to drive into the Grand Canyon and take a thrilling two-day raft ride down a wild section of the Colorado River. The upper portions of Lake Mead penetrate into the Reservation, and motor-boat access is permitted to Separation Canyon via a Reservation road.

Visitors must have a permit before entering any off-highway portion of the Reservation. Permits are available at the Outdoor Recreation office in Peach Springs.

Driving Into the Grand Canyon

The Hualapai Reservation offers the only access into the Grand Canyon by car. You can drive from Peach Springs down Peach Springs Canyon to the inner gorge, at the confluence of Diamond Creek and the Colorado River.

Before the development of *Grand Canyon Village,* which was spurred by the building of a railroad line to that area of the Canyon rim, there was a stagecoach run from Peach Springs to the Diamond Creek/Grand Canyon intersection. Visitors from all over the world made the bone-jarring journey and stayed at the long-since-gone Diamond Creek Hotel, which was within walking distance of the Colorado River.

It is approximately 22 miles via gravel road from Peach Springs to the bottom of Grand Canyon. Getting on the right road to reach the canyon floor is fairly complicated, and visitors are advised to get on-the-spot directions from the Hualapai Wildlife & Outdoor Recreation Department office on Highway 66 in the center of Peach Springs. A small fee is charged for the use of the private road—and for any other use of the Reservation.

Down the Colorado!

The *Hualapai Grand Canyon Outfitters* (also called the R&O River Guides) in Peach Springs, is a tribal venture under the direction of the Wildlife and Outdoor Recreation Department. It offers visitors a one-night, two-day, 54-mile raft trip through the lower gorge of the Grand Canyon on the Colorado River. The trip takes in Diamond Creek Rapids, Travertine Falls, Bridge Canyon Rapids, Spencer Canyon, Surprise Canyon and beautiful Columbine Falls.

These river running expeditions begin at Peach Springs, where the adventurers board a bus (at 9 a.m.) for the 22-mile ride to the bottom of the Grand Canyon. The only thing the "rafter" needs is a sleeping bag and a few personal items. Rental bags are available. Food and the equipment needed are furnished.

The fee for this extraordinary adventure is less than half of what other outfitters charge. If you feel up to going down river this way, call Hualapai Grand Canyon Outfitters at (602) 769-2228, or 769-2227, or write P.O. Box 274, Peach Springs, Arizona 86434 for reservations. A $25.00 deposit per person is needed to confirm reservations.

For those who may want to fly in for this unique experience, package tours are available from either Las Vegas or Grand Canyon Village. A landing strip for personal planes is located at Grand Canyon Caverns, 12 miles west of Peach Springs. Morning pick-up can be arranged. The river-running season is from early April to mid-October.

Fishing & Hunting

There is a limited amount of hunting and fishing on the Hualapai Reservation, and both are closely coordinated with the Arizona State Game and Fish

Department. Information regarding tribal permits for hunting and fishing is available at the Hualapai Wildlife & Outdoor Recreation office. The Reservation has deer, antelope, elk, turkey and bighorn sheep. (Don't miss the mounted heads at the Wildlife office.)

Facilities in Peach Springs

Peach Springs has one motel and a cafeteria. restaurant. The Tribal Visitors Center and Arts and Craft Shop adjoin a general store. Camping and picnic provisions are available at the store, which is open from 8 a.m. to 6 p.m. seven days a week in summer, and Monday through Saturday in winter.

Off Limits!

The western portion of the Hualapai Indian Reservation is off limits to visitors, because the people who live there want to preserve it from the after-effects of tourism.

HAVASUPAI SHANGRI LA

The Havasupai or "People of the Blue-Green Waters," live in the most isolated but also one of the most fascinating of Arizona's Indian Reservations. The center of the Reservation lies at the bottom of Havasu Canyon, a major tributary of the greater Grand Canyon, hundreds of feet below the plateau above.

The peaceful Havasupai, about 300 in number, have lived in this deep, previously unknown canyon since about 1300 A.D., in a setting that the romanticist immediately links with the mystical Shangri La.

Special Note—This section was originally several pages longer, and included detailed information on hiking into and out of Havasu Canyon. The Director of Tourism for the Havasupai tribe asked that the material not be printed because the miniscule size of the canyon and the limited facilities of the tribe make it impossible for them to handle a larger volume of visitors—B.D.

The canyon itself is in part a product of Havasu River, which begins in the upper reaches of the great crevice and makes its way through gorges, trees and Lilliputian bottomlands to the Colorado River in the Grand Canyon.

About midway down Havasu Canyon, an abrupt bulge in its dimensions forms a flat-bottomed, basin-like sanctuary that measures about a mile in length and a third of a mile in width. It is here that the Havasupai live in the village of Supai, surrounded by horse corrals, vegetable gardens, plots of corn and peach trees.

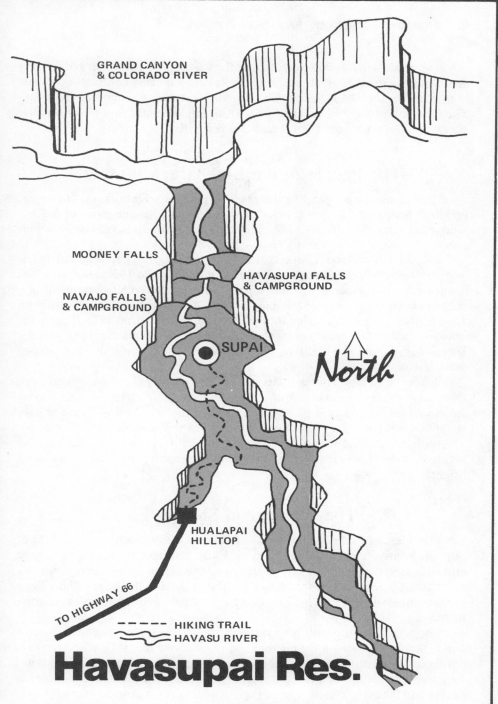

GRAND CANYON
& COLORADO RIVER

MOONEY FALLS

HAVASUPAI FALLS
& CAMPGROUND

NAVAJO FALLS
& CAMPGROUND

SUPAI

North

HUALAPAI
HILLTOP

TO HIGHWAY 66

- - - - - HIKING TRAIL
HAVASU RIVER

Havasupai Res.

(MAP SHOWS ONLY HAVASU CANYON PORTION OF THE RESERVATION)

A short distance down-canyon from the village, Havasu River goes over a series of travertine falls, forming huge pools below that are captivating in their blue-green beauty—and responsible for the picturesque name of the tribe. The falls, in the order of their distance from Supai Village, are Navajo Falls, Havasupai Falls, Mooney Falls and Beaver Falls.

The People of the Blue-Green Waters

The Havasupai people, like their nearby plateau neighbors, the Hualapai, and the Yavapai and Mohave, belong to the Yuman language group of Indians whose ancestral homelands have bordered the Colorado River since ancient times.

Snug in their hidden sanctuary, the Havasupai did not get caught up in the wars between Whites and other Arizona Indians in the 1850s, 60s and 70s. Their beautiful, pocket-canyon homeland, along with small sections of plateau land around the rim of the canyon, was designated as a Reservation on June 8, 1880. The Reservation totaled only 3,055 acres until 1975. That year, an additional 48,000-plus acres were added to the Reservation proper, and the Havasupai gained the right to use another 137,000 acres of surrounding plateau land.

While the isolation of the miniscule Havasupai homeland preserved them from their enemies (and until quite recently from their "friends"), this same isolation and limited area also served to keep the standard of living at subsistence level for a very small population over the generations.

With better health care today and growing income from tourism, the fortunes of the Havasupai have improved considerably, and their future looks bright.

The Weather in Shangri La

The weather in the lower depths of Havasu Canyon and in the village of Supai is relatively mild all year around. Protected from the earliest morning and late afternoon summer sun by trees and the steep, sheer canyon walls— and bathed by cool air descending from the plateau high above—the village escapes most of the torrid heat that is characteristic of other parts of Arizona in July and August.

The same canyon walls also serve to shield Supai from the frigid winter winds that sweep across the higher elevations above them. Daytime temperatures in winter range from the cool 50s to the warm 70s most of the time. Freezing temperatures are common at night during the coldest months. Spring and fall in the canyon are marked by pleasantly warm to fairly hot days, and cool to cold nights.

Visitor Attractions

Visitors are attracted to the *Havasupai Indian Reservation* because of its uniqueness, the bucolic beauty of the canyon, the waterfalls and camping grounds below Supai—and the challenge of getting into and out of the remote reservation.

But the land of "The People of the Blue-Green Waters" is almost as isolated today as it was 100 years ago. There is telephone service from the village to the outside world, however the only way into the canyon hideaway is by helicopter, on foot or horseback. And there is only one foot-and-horse trail into the canyon. This trail begins on the rim of the canyon at a remote access point called *Hualapai Hilltop,* which is at the end of a 67-mile stretch of gravel road that branches off from U.S. 66 a short distance east of Kingman.

Getting There

Campground space and other facilities in Havasu Canyon are strictly limited, and reservations are necessary. To make reservations, call or write the Havasu Tourist Enterprise, Supai, Arizona 86435. Tel. 448-2121. Campgrounds include the Havasupai Campgrounds at Navajo Falls, one-and-a-half miles below Supai; and the National Park Service Campgrounds, two-and-a-half miles below Supai.

The adventure begins with the long drive to Hilltop (see map). The turn-off from U.S. 66 is marked by a sign reading *Supai/Frazier Well.* The latter is about halfway to Hilltop, at an altitude of 6,500 feet. The only facilities at Hilltop, which is on the edge of a branch canyon leading down to Havasu Canyon, are extensive parking areas gouged out of the rugged plateau hills, pit-toilets, horse (and mule) stables operated by the Havasupai tribe, and a telephone linking the jumping off point with Supai.

It is cool to cold at Hilltop during the early morning hours of spring, summer and fall. But inside the upper reaches of the canyon it is hot by 10 a.m. —*very* hot in July and August, because the walls of the canyon and the huge boulders lining its sides radiate heat like micro-wave ovens. (When I and friends hiked into the Canyon, one of our group, a shapely blonde, wore only a red bikini in and out. She also carried a 40-pound backpack, chased *and caught* a foraging Indian pony; and sprinted the last 50 yards up to the rim of the canyon on our way out!)

The first several hundred feet of the journey is almost straight down, via a walkway terraced into the canyon wall in a series of spiraling switch-backs. Near the bottom of the wall, the trail straightens out and proceeds forward at a usually comfortable enough incline, and soon brings you to a normally dry wash-bed which serves more or less as the trail to just above Havasu River.

Once you reach the wash-bed, much of the trail is often not a trail at all in the sense of a well-kept path. There are patches of rocky areas where no trail is discernable, but you can't get lost as long as you don't scale the gorge walls, and keep going down.

Six miles from Hilltop you enter the main body of Havasu Canyon and reach the cool, refreshing waters of Havasu River. The canyon widens at this point, and there are numerous shade trees and underbrush. Supai village is only two miles further on (for a total of eight miles and a 2,000-foot drop in altitude from Hilltop). After you reach the river (creek is more appropriate because it is usually only eight to 20 inches deep and six to 12 feet wide), it is easy to get confused and take the wrong "trail." The village is on the east side of the canyon, while the river runs down the west side, several hundred yards away.

The village of Supai has a short "main street," adjoined by a few buildings and by fenced-in fields. Visitors are required to stop at tribal headquarters, on the right side of the street in a small wooden building, and pay a nominal recreational fee. Supai has a small cafe and a lodge with a limited number of sleeping rooms.

If you prefer to let the horses (or mules) do the walking, you must put your name on the list early and pay in advance in order to get confirmed reservations. Make your reservations by calling the Tourist Manager, Havasu Tourist Enterprise, 448-2121, then sending your money to the same at Supai, Arizona 86435.

Annual Peach Festival

The biggest annual event in the lives of the Havasupai is the *Peach Festival* held each year in August in Supai Village. The occasion includes dancing and horse-racing down "Main Street."

Special Note

Visitors are required to carry all of their own trash and uneaten food supplies out of the canyon to prevent it from becoming one huge garbage pit, and being spoiled for its residents as well as all visitors who come after.

Going Below the Falls

It is possible to reach the Colorado River at the bottom of the Grand Canyon by continuing on down Havasu Canyon beyond the falls. But all semblance of a trail ends just below Mooney Falls, and from there on it is a hard and sometimes dangerous ordeal.

KAIBAB PAIUTE RESERVATION

T he *Kaibab Paiute Indian Reservation,* located on the Markagunt Plateau "behind" Grand Canyon National Park and Kaibab National Forest, is the most remote from Arizona's population centers. The northern boundary of the Reservation adjoins Utah. It is accessible via paved highway only from Utah on the north, and from Arizona's Jacob Lake on the east.

Most of the Reservation, which encompasses 120,413 acres, is fairly level ground with a covering of scrub brush and juniper trees. The terrain is occasionally broken by draws and rather spectacular cliffs.

There are fewer than 200 Paiute residents on the Reservation, the majority of which live in the village of Kaibab, about 12 miles west of Fredonia, Arizona, the only town nearby. The Kaibab Paiutes are members of the large Paiute tribal group that in pre-White-man days were nomadic wanderers, and now mostly live in other states.

Visitor Attractions

The only visitor attraction of any note on the Paiute Reservation is the famous *Pipe Spring National Monument,* a fort built by Mormons in 1870 to protect settlers from marauding Indians coming up from the central and eastern portions of Arizona.

The great spring, around which the fort was built, consists of two pools flowing from the Sevier Fault on Moccasin Terrace, in an area popularly called "The Arizona Strip" near the southern end of an escarpment known as Vermilion Cliffs.

The fort was originally called *Winsor Castle,* and was never attacked by Indians. It served as a ranch house until 1923, when it was designated a National Monument. The Monument is on Highway 389 near Kaibab village, some 15 miles west of Fredonia.

A Visitor's Center, museum, handicraft gift shop and a snackbar adjoin the Monument headquarters. There is also a 45-unit trailer park, with all hook-ups, near the headquarter facilities. (The most distinctive Paiute handicraft available at the gift shop is a coiled, shallow basket known as a "Wedding Basket.")

The National Park Service administers the monument, and provides daily guide service for visitors, from 8 a.m. to 4:30 p.m. Deep snowfalls are common in the Kaibab area in January and February, but the highway to the monument is kept open. Snow-chains are advisable during these months, however. Elevation in the vicinity of the monument is about 5,000 feet.

THREE

Mountain Reservations

WHITE MOUNTAIN APACHE LAND

The *Fort Apache Indian Reservation,* established on June 7, 1897 for the White Mountain Apaches, was originally a part of the "White Mountain San Carlos Indian Reservation," where several of Arizona's Apache Indian tribes were confined together. Situated in the scenic wonderland of the White Mountains in northeast-central Arizona, some 150 miles from Metropolitan Phoenix, the Reservation has been called "the largest privately owned recreational area in the U.S."

Altogether, the Fort Apache Reservation includes 1,664,872 acres, made up of scrub-covered low hills and valleys in the southwestern portion, and heavily forested mountains, high meadows and deep canyons in the northern and eastern portions.

The Reservation is bordered on the west by the Tonto National Forest; on the north by Sitgreaves National Forest; on the east by the Apache National Forest; and on the south by the San Carlos Indian Reservation. Great areas of White Mountain Apache Land are forested, with stands of ponderosa pine, spruce, fir and aspen in the higher elevations; and pinion, juniper and sycamore on lower mountain slopes and stream banks.

Highest point on the Reservation is Mt. Baldy on the eastern border, which rises to an impressive 11,459 feet. The lowest elevation is 2,700 feet in Salt River Canyon.

The People of the White Mountains

The White Mountain Apache Indians who live on the Fort Apache Reservation call themselves *Di Neh,* or "The People," in their native tongue.

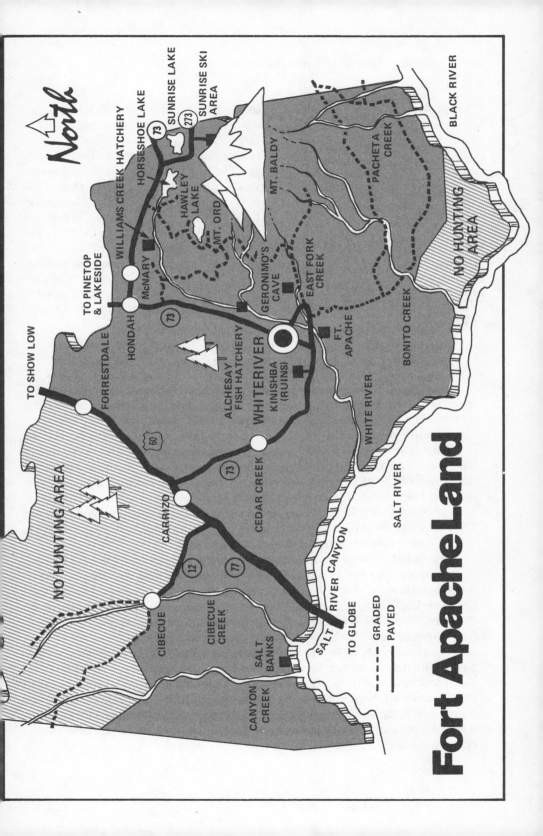

Fort Apache Land

One of Arizona's most independent and formidable Indian tribes, their numbers had been reduced to around 2,000 when the Reservation was established. Now they number over 6,000.

The Ft. Apache Reservation owes its name indirectly to Cochise, one of Arizona's most famous tribal chieftains. The first fort to be established in the heartland of the White Mountain Apache tribe was called Camp Ord. This was later changed to Camp Thomas in honor of Gen. George W. Thomas of Civil War fame. It was finally named Ft. Apache as a goodwill gesture toward Cochise, who visited the camp for several weeks in 1870. When the reservation was created it became the Fort Apache Indian Reservation.

Ft. Apache itself was manned until 1924, when it was turned over to the Bureau of Indian Affairs to be used as a school for Indian children. Many of the buildings of the old fort still stand. The quarters of one of its earlier commanders, Gen. George Crook, is now a museum operated by the *Apache Cultural Center*.

The Turning Point

Until the 1950s the Fort Apache Indian Reservation was mostly isolated from the rest of the world. Most areas of the Reservation were accessible only by horseback or on foot, over the most primitive trails. The people had little contact with the outside.

Then after months of deliberation, progressive tribal leaders agreed that if they were ever going to make the tribe economically viable and at the same time preserve its identity and heritage, extraordinary and bold actions were needed. They decided to develop the beautiful mountains, meadows, valleys and streams of their Reservation into a recreation and vacation wonderland. They adopted the Apache word *Hon-Dah,* meaning "Welcome" or "Be My Guest," as symbolic of this new policy and enterprise.

The program began with the construction of numerous access roads. Next came a number of high-altitude dams that formed a series of lakes, including Hawley, Pacheta, Hurricane, Drift Fence, Cooley, Horseshoe, Cienega, Earl Park, Christmas Tree, Bootleg, Sunrise, A-1, Cyclone, Sush Bezahze, Shush Be Toue, Bog, East and West Blue Lakes, George's Basin— plus dozens of smaller lakes or ponds, often called "tanks."

Then campsites were constructed around the lakes and along many of the mountain streams on the Reservation—White River and its two tributaries Northfork and Eastfork; Big and Little Diamond, Big and Little Bonito, Paradise, Trout, Snake, Becker, Cibicue, Black River, and others. Completion of campgrounds was followed by the construction of motels, cabins, boat docks, stores, service stations and other facilities designed to serve the needs of large numbers of visitors.

MOUNTAIN RESERVATIONS   69

In their construction program, the White Mountain Apaches took special care to make sure that the natural scenic beauty of the Reservation was preserved. Once the construction phase was completed, they then promulgated a series of rules and regulations designed to further protect the Reservation and ensure that the new facilities would be properly used.

In addition to its tourist industry, directed by the White Mountain Apache Recreation Enterprise, a corporation wholly owned by the tribe, the White Mountain Apaches are also noted cattle-raisers, and operate a thriving lumber business.

The larger of the towns and communities on the Reservation are Whiteriver, the tribal headquarters, McNary and Cibecue. Cibecue, ancestral homeland of the Cibecue Apaches in the west-central portion of the reservation, retains much of the flavor of Apache life before the turn of the century.

The Weather

As always in Arizona, the most important thing to keep in mind about the weather on Ft. Apache Reservation is the altitude first and the season second. Elevation on the reservation has a spread of nearly 9,000 feet, enough to produce changes in climate and vegetation that is the equivalent of a trip from New Orleans to southern Canada.

Temperature changes between day and night are dramatic in the summer as well as the winter. In the highest elevations of the Reservation, winter temperatures range from as low as 20 or more below zero at night to 50 or 60 degrees above zero during the day. During summer, the daytime termperatures at higher elevations are in the cool 60s, 70s and 80s; dropping as many as 30 degrees at night. Daytime summer temperatures in the narrow confines of the Salt River Canyon often soar above 100, with only a slight cooling at night. In winter, the same location has cold nights and cool to balmy days.

The Fabulous Sunrise Resort

Sunrise Resort Park, on the eastern edge of White Mountain Apache Land, between Show Low and Springerville and 24 miles from McNary, is the most elaborate and impressive recreational complex on any of Arizona's Indian Reservations, and the centerpiece of Fort Apache Reservation's many attractions.

Situated in a large vale near the summit of Mt. Ord and looking up at Mt. Baldy, highest point on the Reservation, the complex includes the most beautiful and best ski resort in the state, a plush year-around resort hotel, a well-stocked fishing and boating lake, miles of riding and hiking trails, and numerous camping sites.

Headquarters for many of the summer and winter visitors to the resort complex is Sunrise Hotel, which is perched on a ridge overlooking Sunrise Lake, and offers its guests first-class accommodations-plus-entertainment in a magnificent mountain-wilderness setting. The hotel has 106 rooms and suites, an excellent dining room, coffee shop, convention facilities, Indian craft shop, gift shop, cocktail lounge, sauna bath and sunlamps, plus a children's play area and a large attractive lobby.

For those who like an added touch of privacy and exclusivity, there are two-story 3-bedroom chalets set amidst huge pine trees on a knoll less than 100 yards from the hotel. All of the chalets face Sunrise Lake, and have floor-to-ceiling glass walls in front. Each of the chalets is designed to accommodate as many as three families (who can share expenses) during the peak winter-skiing and summer-recreational seasons.

Other facilities being added to the hotel complex include tennis courts, an indoor pool for year-around swimming, and a new convention hall that will accommodate 300 persons.

Facilities at Sunrise Lake already in existence or abuilding, include a fully equipped boat marina and 48 floating boat-slips. Boats using the lake are limited to those with sails or electric motors with a maximum of three horse-power. The lake has its winter as well as summer enthusiasts—the former including those who enjoy ice-skating and ice-fishing.

Of course, the biggest wintertime attraction at Sunrise are the 16 ski-runs, served by a 6,780-foot Heron-Poma double chairlift, a 1,604-ft. double chair-lift, and a rope-tow. Altogether, the lifts have a moving capacity of 2,000 skiers per hour—which works out to over 33 per minute!

The large lodge at the base of the ski area includes a cafeteria, bar, a ski rental shop, a sporting goods shop, and a ski school that is staffed by nationally certified instructors (up to 45 during the height of the season!). The sundeck of the lodge provides a good view of the ski-runs, plus the "School Corral" and "Fanny Hill" where beginners get their first taste of this very unique experience.

When the Skiing Season Begins

Thanksgiving Day is traditionally the beginning of the skiiing season at Sunrise. The peak season is from 19 December through 5 January—and anyone who wants hotel or chalet accommodations during this period should reserve (and pay!) months in advance.

Weekends are, of course, the busiest at Sunrise Ski Resort, so it makes a lot of sense to go during the week if you can. In fact, Sunrise Hotel offers a series of special "mid-week ski packages" that are available from Sunday night through Thursday night, with the exceptions of November 27 and 28, and December 19 through January 5.

There are three categories of the mid-week ski packages: Novice, Intermediate and Advanced. All are available on a one-night or three-night basis. A Novice three-nighter includes lodgings for three nights, ski equipment for three days, a 3-day lift pass and three lessons—and all of this for less than what you would expect to pay for a room only in some Las Vegas Hotels for example. The fee for those who bring their own equipment and do not need or want lessons—the Advanced category—costs approximately one-third less than the Novice category. All prices are on a per person basis with double room occupancy—which means if you don't have a mate or close friend, you have to find one!

There is regular bus transportation from Sunrise Hotel to the ski lodge and slopes, three miles away.

Besides season-opening festivities on Thanksgiving Day, which features a large family-style dinner, the skiing season is marked by a number of annual events, including a Christmas Day party, a Washington's Birthday party, and a *Winter-Fest* on the last weekend in February that includes four types of racing competition open to all.

On the last weekend of the skiing season, there is an annual *Slush Cup Race*, which consists of the professionals on the staff coming down off a run and trying to ski across a once-frozen-over pond.

Spring events at the Hotel complex include such things as an *All-Indian Arts & Crafts Show* over Memorial Day weekend. During the summer months there are nearby rodeos almost every weekend, with the largest on the 4th of July and Labor Day weekends.

Winter-time entertainment at Sunrise Resort Hotel includes ski movies, ski fashion shows, regular lounge musical groups, and sometimes Apache Indian Crown Dancers.

Many Arizona residents seem to be under the impression that the Sunrise Resort Complex is *only* a ski resort, open only in the winter. It is very definitely a 4-season recreational center, with action going on all year around. With summer daytime temperatures from 20 to 30 degrees below those in most of the central and southern areas of the state, some people drive up just to get a reprieve from the heat and breathe some tangy mountain air—or to enjoy the turning of the aspens in late September and early October.

Then there are the lakes for fishing and boating, miles of hills and meadows for horseback riding and hiking . . . and a sense of being especially alive and in harmony with the world.

For reservations at Sunrise Hotel, call 1-334-2144 or write P.O. Box 217, McNary, Arizona 85930. A deposit is required before reservations can be held.

Sightseeing Attractions

Besides the outstanding beauty of it all, White Mountain Apache Land boasts a number of specific sightseeing attractions. The major ones:

Alchesay National Fish Hatchery—Five miles north of Whiteriver in Whiteriver Canyon, the Alchesay Hatchery is ranked as one of the most scenic and modern fish-culture stations in the U.S. A *Visitor Center* and picnic grounds adjoin the hatchery. The Center is open from 8 a.m. to 5 p.m. daily.

Fort Apache—Established in 1870 during the Indian Wars, Ft. Apache played a leading role in bringing peace with the Navajo and Apache Indians. The fort was headquarters for the famous *Apache Scouts,* who were primarily responsible for hunting down and helping to subdue the last bands of renegade Apaches and Navajos in the 1870s and 80s. Many of the original buildings of the fort are still standing. It is located on a loop of Highway 73 a few minutes south of Whiteriver. General George Crook's quarters, built in 1883, is now a museum. Visitors are welcomed.

Ft. Apache Timber Mill—Lumbering is one of the Big Three industries on the Ft. Apache Reservation. This Apache-owned and operated mill is just south of Whiteriver. Visitors are welcomed.

Geronimo's Cave—About six miles east of Ft. Apache on the East Fork of White River, this large, dry cave was reputedly used by Geronimo as a hideout when he was being hunted by the U.S. cavalry. It is now a popular visitor stop-over. See map for location.

Hawley Lake—A sight to see as well as a recreational area, Hawley is one of the best-known Apache Land lakes. It is 8,500 feet above sea level, in a forest of ponderosa pine, fir, spruce and quaking aspen.

There are more than 100 camping sites spaced around the 7½ miles of shoreline, and a number of visitor and fishermen facilities, including rental cabins, a large boat dock, grocery store, trailer park and riding stables—all operated by Apache Indians. There are also 500 or so homesite lots along the shores of the lake, leased to vacationers for summer and winter cabins.

Kinishba ("The Brown House")—The Ft. Apache Reservation is dotted with ruins left by Indians who occupied the area before the coming of the Apaches—Indians who lived in "apartments" or "condominiums" and had relatively sophisticated life-styles. The largest of these apartment complex ruins is called *Kinishba,* or "The Brown House," by the Apaches.

Actually a village consisting of two huge apartment complexes with more than 200 rooms each, plus several smaller detached buildings with an additional 400 to 500 ground-floor rooms, *Kinishba* is believed to have been founded around 700 A.D., and to have reached its peak during the 1200s when it had a population of about 2,000. The village was abandoned completely sometime after 1350 A.D., apparently because the water source failed.

About eight miles southwest of Whiteriver, a few minutes off of Highway 73, *Kinishba* is a Registered National Historic Landmark.

McNary Lumber Mill—This is a large sawmill operated by Southwest Forest Industries in McNary. The operators of the mill offer a visitor's tour of the plant every weekday, beginning at 12:30 p.m., from Memorial Day in the spring to Labor Day in the fall. Experienced guides explain each operation of the lumber business, from tree to finished product. The mill is visible from the highway.

Salt Banks—Seven miles downstream from the bridge where U.S. Highway 60 crosses the Salt River in Salt River Canyon, these spectacular salt banks are said to have been sacred to the Apaches, and a source of salt for both Indians and early Spanish and American settlers. The banks are accessible via a paved road from the Salt River Bridge.

Salt River—The Ft. Apache Reservation is the primary birthplace of the Salt River, the key lifeline of Metropolitan Phoenix. The river begins as numerous streams in the 12,000-foot mountain ranges on the eastern edge of the Reservation. These streams merge in turn to form White River and Black River. Some 20 miles southwest of Ft. Apache, these two rivers join and become the Salt River, which passes through the sculptured gorges of Salt River Canyon to end up in the homes and on the lawns, gardens and farms of residents of the Valley of the Sun.

Father Eusebio Kino, the intrepid missionary-explorer who visited the area in 1698, is credited with having given the river its present-day name— either from the salt cedars that line its shores further down, or the huge salt banks and caves at the point where Cibecue Creek enters the larger stream.

Salt River Canyon—Not as breathtaking as the Grand Canyon because it is not as deep or as wide, the Salt River Canyon in many ways is just as beautiful as the larger, more famous canyon. Its special advantage is that you can drive through it, and get close-up views of its extraordinary scenic beauty. There are a number of lookout points with plenty of parking space along U.S. 60, which passes through the canyon.

Williams Creek Hatchery—Just below Blue Lake at the confluence of Williams Creek and North Fork (between Whiteriver and McNary), the Williams Creek Hatchery produces over 100,000 pounds of rainbow trout each year. Most of the young trout are transplanted to Reservation streams and lakes, for the benefit of fishermen, when they are nine inches long. The hatchery is open daily from 8 a.m. to 5 p.m.

Annual Events

Sunrise Dance (Puberty Rites)—The *Nah-ih-es,* which literally means "Preparing her" or "Getting her ready," is the traditional Coming of Age ritual for Apache daughters, and is popularly known as the *Sunrise Dance*. The ceremony, once the major event in every Apache girl's life, is now staged for only a few girls each year because of the growing expense of the fees and gifts involved, and because many of the daughters and their parents no longer feel comfortable following the old ways.

The puberty ceremonies that are staged usually take place during the annual tribal fair and rodeo in Whiteriver, which are generally held over a 3-day period at the end of August and the first of September.

The ceremony of *Nah-ih-es* does not mean that the girl is expected to get married soon afterward. The main purpose of the ritual is to ensure that the girl will enjoy good health, strength, prosperity, a good disposition, a long life, and have many friends to the end of her days.

There are several parts to the Sunrise ceremony, including some in which medicine men, singers and *gahns* (masked dancers) participate. Before the ceremony, the daughters are referred to as "girls." Afterward they are regarded as women. For four days following the ritual, the newly initiated young women are believed to possess some of the powers attributed to the *gahn*. They are believed to be able to heal, bring good luck, bless babies and even influence the weather.

Key figures in traditional and sacred Apache ceremonies, the *gahn*, masked dancers personifying tribal deities, are believed to have miraculous powers during the ceremonies—powers that enable them to cure physical and mental illnesses and do other extraordinary things.

Before a sacred rite or healing session, the men designated as *gahn* go through periods of meditation and purification. The *gahn* dancers are said to be especially effective in curing psychosomatic illnesses and complaints having to do with cultural alienation. Whatever the power of the *gahns*, their dances affect even white spectators, bringing to some of them a sense of well-being, peace and inner harmony that lasts as long as one is in Apache Land.

Visitors are welcomed as spectators at the Sunrise Dance puberty rituals, and may take photographs by obtaining permission in advance.

Cedar Creek Pow Wow—Generally held on the second weekend in June of each year, this popular event includes a rodeo and carnival. A number of ceremonial dances are also usually part of the main attraction.

Independence Day Celebration—A rodeo, ceremonial dances, barbecues and other festivities mark this 4th of July celebration at the Ft. Apache Reservation tribal headquarters in Whiteriver.

Tribal Fair & Rodeo—Held in Whiteriver on Labor Day weekend each year, the annual tribal fair and rodeo is the main Ft. Apache Reservation event. Besides the rodeo (in which all of the participants are Apache cowboys), handicraft and food booths, the event is also the occasion for the presentation of traditional Apache Indian dances, including the famous Crown Dance and the Sunrise "puberty ritual" Dance.

Cattle Roundup & Auction—Every October the Old West comes alive again on the Ft. Apache Indian Reservation when Apache cowboys round up the tribal cattle herds and drive them to Whiteriver stockyards for the annual auction. Thousands of Arizona residents and visitors take advantage of the opportunity to combine witnessing a page out of the past and enjoying a weekend in the high country with its pine-perfumed air and multi-colored leaves of fall. The auctions take place every Tuesday in October.

During July and August there are ceremonial dances in and in the vicinity of Whiteriver every weekend. None of these events are "scheduled" but visitors can usually find one or more of them by inquiring locally.

The Fisherman's Haven

The Ft. Apache Indian Reservation is the largest "fishing preserve" in Arizona. The Reservation has some 400 miles of mountain streams regularly stocked with rainbow and brown trout to assure fishermen of a good catch—not to mention several dozen man-made lakes and ponds or "tanks."

All visitors and non-Apaches over the age of 14 must have a valid Arizona fishing license, an Arizona "trout stamp" and an Apache Reservation fishing permit in their possession while fishing on the Reservation. The trout limit is 10 fish per day. Youngsters under the age of 14 may fish on the Ft. Apache Reservation without licenses or permits if they are accompanied by an adult with valid licenses and permits. Non-licensed youths may take or have in their possession only half the trout limit set for licensed fishermen.

Live bait is prohibited on all waters of the Reservation at all times. Anyone caught with live bait will be removed from the Reservation, and barred for a period of eight years. Offenders may also be fined.

An agreement between the White Mountain Apaches and San Carlos Apaches allows holders of valid permits from either Reservation to fish either side of the Black and Salt Rivers where these rivers form the boundary line between the two reservations.

For locations of the primary rivers and lakes on the Reservation, see the accompanying map. Christmas Tree and Hurricane Lakes are very shallow and are designated as "walk-in" lakes. Christmas Tree Lake is stocked only with native trout, and is subject to special regulations and permit fees. These special permits and regulations are available from the White Mountain Recreation Enterprise office in Whiteriver.

Among the largest and most popular lakes on the Reservation are Hawley and Horseshoe. Hawley Lake, often in the news as Arizona's coolest in-habited spot in the summer and coldest spot in the winter, is at an elevation of 8,500 feet. Summer afternoon temperatures around the lake are usually in the 60s and 70s. At night the thermometer drops into the 40s and sometimes 30s.

Afternoon showers are commonplace in July and August. Hawley is about 15 miles southeast of McNary, via Highways 73 and 473.

Hawley Lake has 100 campsites, rental cabins, a horseback riding stable and several other visitor facilities. The season begins in May and lasts through October.

Horseshoe Lake, a few minutes east of Hawley, is 8,200 feet high and has a slightly milder climate than Hawley Lake. Facilities here include a boat dock, rental boats and a store. Afternoon showers in July and August are also daily occurrences.

Reservation fishing permits are available from the White Mountain Apache Enterprise office in Whiteriver, and from various trading posts and stores around the Reservation. See a list of locations following the section on hunting.

Camping in White Mountain Apache Land

There are over 700 camp and picnic sites scattered throughout the White Mountain Apache Reservation. These sites are in especially scenic areas along streams and on the banks of lakes, in canyons, and on mountain tops. They are provided with tables, barbecue fireplaces, toilets, trash containers or pits; and most of them have drinking water. Camping is permitted in the vicinity of all lakes on the reservation except Cyclone, Christmas Tree and Hurricane Lakes.

Reservations are not required at any of these locations, and visitors—with camping permits—are invited to make use of any unoccupied site. A set of rules is posted at each camp. Game wardens and Reservation rangers regularly patrol the areas.

Camping permits, sold at a nominal cost, must be prominently displayed at all times so that they can be inspected by Reservation rangers. Most campers place the permits in the windows of their vehicles, so they are readily visible from the outside.

Campgrounds at Hawley Lake, Horseshoe, Cienega, Bog Tank and Sunrise Lake have piped spring water. Most other campgrounds on the Reservation have spring water in the vicinity. Campgrounds are visited regularly by clean-up crews, but campers and picnickers are expected to clean up after themselves.

Rules for Visitors

To prevent their Reservation from being turned into a wasteland of garbage by unconscionable visitors, the White Mountain Apaches have established the following rules for campers, fishermen, hunters and picnickers:

1) Don't litter the streams, campgrounds or roadsides. Disposal of all forms of waste on the ground from campers, trailers, mobile homes, etc., is prohibited except at authorized disposal areas. Violators will be prohibited from either fishing or camping on the Reservation for a period of five years.

2) All trash is to be put into containers provided for that purpose at campgrounds and picnic sites. Dumping of cans, bottles, plastic bags, etc., into vault-type toilets is expressly prohibited because these toilets must be pumped out and it is impossible to do so if they are clogged with junked containers.

3) Do not clean fish in the springs, streams or lakes of the Reservation.

4) Do not destroy or deface signs, tables or improvements anywhere on the Reservation.

5) Use only dead trees and downed timber for your campfires.

6) No firearms are permitted in the field without a valid hunting permit.

7) Camping is limited to posted campgrounds.

8) Gasoline engines are not permitted on any Reservation lake.

9) Swimming is not permitted in any Reservation lake except where posted.

10) Boats are not allowed on either Big or Little Blue Lake.

11) Some streams are closed, and are posted.

(The upper reaches of several streams on the Ft. Apache Reservation are closed, and carefully marked, to protect and preserve the spawning grounds of the rainbow and brown trout that populate the several hundred miles of fishing waters.

Major Campgrounds On the Reservation

Name of Area	Elevation	Location	Trailers OK	Safe Water	No. of Units	Fishing	Boating	Season	Days
A-1 Lake	8,000 ft	16 mi. E. McNary	x	x	4	x		May–Nov.	10
Alchesay Springs	5,800	7 mi. N. Whiteriver	x	x	10	x		Apr.–Nov.	10
Bog Creek	7,400	13 mi. E. McNary	x	x	5	x	x	Apr.–Nov.	10
Bootleg Lake	7,000	4 mi. S. McNary	x		15	x	x	Apr.–Nov.	10
Cibecue Creek	6,000	40 mi. E. Whiteriver	x	x	10	x		All year	10
Cooley Lake	7,000	4 mi. E. McNary	x	x	10	x	x	Apr.–Nov.	10
Cyclone Lake	9,000	28 mi. NE Whiteriver				x		Walk-in	
Diamond Creek Jct.	5,500	3 mi. N. Whiteriver	x	x	10	x		Apr.–Nov.	10
Diamond Creek 2	5,600	6 mi. NE Whiteriver	x	x	7	x		Apr.–Nov.	10
Diamond Creek 3	6,000	10 mi. NE Whiteriver	x	x	10	x		Apr.–Nov.	10
Diamond Creek 4	7,500	15 mi. NE Whiteriver	x	x	5	x		Apr.–Nov.	10
Diamond Creek 5	8,000	23 mi. NE Whiteriver	x	x	3	x		Apr.–Nov.	10
Ditch Camp, N. Fork	7,600	15 mi. E. McNary	x	x	15	x		Apr.–Nov.	10
Drift Fence Lake	8,000	10 mi. N. Maverick	x	x	3	x	x	Apr.–Nov.	10
East Fork	6,000	10 mi. E. Whiteriver	x	x	15	x		Apr.–Nov.	10
Hawley Lake	8,500	30 mi. NE Whiteriver	x	x	100	x	x	All year	10
Horseshoe Cienega Lake	8,200	10 mi. E. McNary	x	x	30	x	x	Apr.–Nov.	10
Hurricane Lake Walk-in	9,000	12 mi. N. Maverick				x		Apr.–Nov.	
Lower Big Bonito	6,000	13 mi. SE Whiteriver	x	x	2	x		Apr.–Nov.	10
Lower Diamond Cr.	5,500	3½ mi. N. Whiteriver	x	x	12	x		Apr.–Nov.	10
Lower Log Rd.	6,500	13 mi. N. Whiteriver	x	x	100	x		Apr.–Nov.	10
McCoy's Bridge	7,400	12 mi. E. McNary	x	x	20	x		Apr.–Nov.	10
Pacheta Lake	8,500	2½ N. Maverick	x	x	15	x		Apr.–Nov.	10
Reservation Lake	9,500	10 mi. NE Maverick	x	x	40	x	x	Apr.–Nov.	10
Rock Creek	6,000	13 mi. E. Whiteriver	x	x	2	x	x	Apr.–Nov.	10
Ryan Ranch	7,600	15 mi. E. McNary	x	x	5	x		Apr.–Nov.	10
Salt River Canyon	3,000	45 W. Whiteriver	x	x	8	x		All year	10
Shush-Be-Tou Lake	7,600	10 mi. E. McNary	x	x	10	x	x	May–Nov.	10
Shush-Bezazhe Lake	7,500	10 mi. E. McNary	x	x	6	x	x	May–Nov.	10
Sunrise Lake	9,000	24 mi. E. McNary	x	x	200	x	x	All year	10
Upper Big Bonito	6,000	15 SE Whiteriver	x	x	2	x	x	Apr.–Nov.	10

Hunting in White Mountain Apache Land

The Fort Apache Indian Reservation abounds in many kinds of wildlife, and hunting by non-Indians is permitted in seasons which normally coincide with those set by the Arizona Game and Fish Commission for public areas of the state. Two major areas of the Reservation are barred to all hunting by non-Apaches, however, and special care should be taken to avoid these districts. One is a large section in the northwestern portion of the Reservation, and the other is a smaller section on the southeastern tip. See the Ft. Apache Reservation map.

Among the game animals that may be hunted on the Reservation by non-Indians are elk, antelope, bear, javelina and mountain lion. Only Fort Apache Indians are allowed to hunt turkey and deer on the Reservation. Licenses for hunting elk on the Reservation are issued in a drawing conducted by the Arizona Game & Fish Department in Phoenix, usually in the fall.

Where to Get Permits

Permits for camping, fishing and hunting on the Fort Apache Indian Reservation are available from numerous dealers around the state and on the reservation. Among them:

ALPINE
The Tackle Shop

CIBECUE
Cibecue Trading Co.

CARRIZO
Carrizo Junction
Carrizo Store

CLIFTON
S & S Sporting Goods

COOLIDGE
H&H Hardware

GLOBE
A.J. Bayless Market
Unique Sporting Goods
Yellow Front

GREER
F-Bar-K & Cafe
George Crosby's
Leads Northwoods Lodge

HAWLEY LAKE
Hawley Lake Store
Boat Docks

HOLBROOK
Western Auto Store

HON-DAH
Service Station & Store

LAKESIDE
Lakeside Circle A
Little Big Bear

McNARY
General Store
Liquor Store

MIAMI
United Jewelry Co.

PHOENIX
Angler's Roost
Camelback Gun Shop
Gemco

The Gun Room
Yates Stores

PINETOP
Collings Auto Supplies
Pinetop Lakes Dept.
Bob Weete's

SALT RIVER CANYON
Salt River Canyon
  Station

SCOTTSDALE
Don's Sport Shop

SHOW LOW
Ace Store
Show Low Surplus

SNOWFLAKE
Kay's Sporting Goods

SPRINGERVILLE
Big Lake Tackle
Sport Shack

Alfred's Sporting Goods
  & Western Wear
**SUNRISE RESORT
  PARK**
Sunrise Hotel

TUCSON
Cash Box
Joe's Eastside Tackle &
  Supply
F. Ronstadt Hardware

WHITERIVER
Apache Service Station
White Mt. Apache
  Enterprise
Whiteriver Trading Co.

Taking Pictures

Visitors are permitted to take photographs of all spectator and public events on the Fort Apache Indian Reservation. But permission should be obtained before photographing private individuals, parties, groups, private residences or any activity taking place on private property.

Other Sights to See

In addition to the natural beauty and special attractions of Fort Apache Reservation, White Mountain Apache Land adjoins or is near other areas with outstanding scenic and recreational attractions.

The northwestern boundary of the Reservation is formed by one of the planet earth's most impressive geographic features—the famous *Mogollon Rim*. This is a remarkable escarpment that drops off suddenly for nearly half a mile, and separates the plateau regions of northern Arizona from the lower central and southern desert areas. This extraordinary sight is accessible from the south via Payson, and from the north via Show Low and Heber.

The *White Mountain Scenic Railroad* is another major attraction in the vicinity of the Fort Apache Reservation. The circa 1880s steam-powered train, stationed at a picturesque depot just south of Pinetop near the Reservation line, makes one roundtrip each weekday and two on weekends through some of the most scenic alpine mountain country in the world.

Overnight Accommodations

Hotel/motel accommodations on the Fort Apache Indian Reservation are presently limited to the plush Sunrise Resort Hotel at Sunrise, and the Hon-Dah Motel, near McNary at the junction of Highways 73 and 173. The Hon Dah Motel complex includes 10 motel rooms, two duplex cabins, and 13 single-unit detached cabins among tall pines; plus a restaurant, grocery store, cocktail lounge and service station.

For reservations at the Hon-Dah, write Box 597, McNary, Arizona 85930, or call 336-4311.

There are numerous visitor facilities in the several alpine towns near the Fort Apache Reservation, particularly at Show Low, Pinetop, Greer and Springerville.

SAN CARLOS APACHE LAND

The *San Carlos Indian Reservation*, in east-central Arizona, was established on November 9, 1871 and December 14, 1872, for several different Apache bands, along with groups of other Arizona Indians. Disregarding the welfare of the Indians—along with the traditional enmity that existed between the various tribes—the authorities chose to crowd several of the bands together for the sake of convenience.

The Reservation, then sometimes called the "White Mountain San Carlos Indian Reservation," included some of the area that is now the Fort Apache Reservation, homeland of the White Mountain Apaches, plus several million acres to the east and north. But great sections of the Reservation were then systematically sliced off and returned to the public domain, by Executive Order, on eight different occasions between 1873 and 1902, leaving the Reservation approximately one-third of its original size.

The first years of the Reservation's history were anything but quiet and peaceful. The overcrowded conditions quickly led to friction between the different tribes. The Apaches had had limited farming experience and did not take to it readily. To make matters worse, there was wholesale cheating by the white agents assigned to provide the penned up Indians with food and supplies.

This volatile situation led several of the war chiefs confined on the Reservation to begin a series of raids on Arizona and Sonora, Mexico communities that kept the territory in an uproar for some 15 years. Among the more famous of these war chiefs were Cochise, Victoria, Geronimo, Natiotish, Juh, Nolgee and Chatto.

The authorities finally moved the Mohave, Chiricahua Apaches, Warm Springs Apaches and Yuma Indians to other Reservations, but the raids by the dissatisfied war chiefs did not end until they were all killed, or captured and exiled. The last one to surrender was Geronimo, who gave up for the last time in September 1886, and was quickly shipped off to a prisoner-of-war camp in Florida. Real peace was not achieved on the Reservation until 1897, when it was divided between the San Carlos Apaches and the White Mountain Apaches, with the northern portion where most of the White Mountain Apaches lived being designated as the Fort Apache Indian Reservation.

The San Carlos Reservation that remained had a total of 1,853,841 acres, and was still the fourth largest of Arizona's Indian reservations. The San Carlos, especially in the northern and northeastern sectors, also rivals the Fort Apache Reservation and the Navajo Nation in the scenic beauty of its mountains, canyons, cienegas, lakes and streams—and its potential as a recreational area.

Elevation on the San Carlos Reservation ranges from 2,400 feet at San Carlos Lake in the southwest portion, to 7,874 feet in the northeast corner.

The average altitude is between 5,000 and 6,000 feet, tempering the heat of the summer sun and limiting the cold of the winter.

The Reservation has three distinct categories of terrain. The southwest portion is made up of picturesque desert highlands with low, rolling hills and mazes of arroyos and gulches. The central portion of the Reservation consists of alternating mountain ridges and mile-high meadows that are covered with grass and wild flowers during the spring and summer months. The northeastern section of the Reservation is primarily high mountains and plateau country, with forests of blue spruce, pine and aspen.

The northern, central and eastern portions of the Reservation are also marked by a number of rugged, scenic canyons that are characteristic of large areas of Arizona. These include Cottonwood Canyon, Sawmill Canyon, Wild Horse Canyon, Bronco Canyon, Popcorn Canyon, Tanks Canyon and Bear Canyon.

Also like other mountainous areas in Arizona, San Carlos is noted for its man-made lakes, the larger of which result in a startling contrast between their deep blue water and the starkness of the surrounding desert-canyon country.

Besides its lakes and over 100 ponds, the northeastern section of the San Carlos Reservation is laced by a network of cool, swift mountain creeks that provide additional miles of fishing waters. The northern boundary of the Reservation is formed by over 50 miles of the combined Black and Salt Rivers (one of Arizona's major river systems), which are shared in common with the adjoining Fort Apache Indian Reservation.

Largest and best known of the Reservation lakes is *San Carlos Lake,* formed by the equally famous Coolidge Dam, just south of Peridot on the Reservation, via Highway 70 (and only 25 miles southeast of Globe on U.S. 60). Other popular lakes on the Reservation include *Seneca* in the northwest corner near U.S. 60 and the Salt River Canyon Bridge, and *Point of Pines Lake* in the east central sector of the Reservation, near the junctures of Routes 4, 14, 15 and 17.

The San Carlos Apaches

The San Carlos Apaches today are a peaceful, progressive and industrious people, engaging in cattle-raising, lumbering, mining and tourism. They are often called the "Cowboy Indians of the West" not only because large numbers of them are in the cattle business, but also because they dress like, look like and act like cowboys.

Huge sections of the Reservation were used as grazing lands by non-Indian cattle companies until 1933, when their leases and grazing permits were cancelled to give the San Carlos Apaches an opportunity to get into the cattle business. Today there are five associations of cattle raisers on the

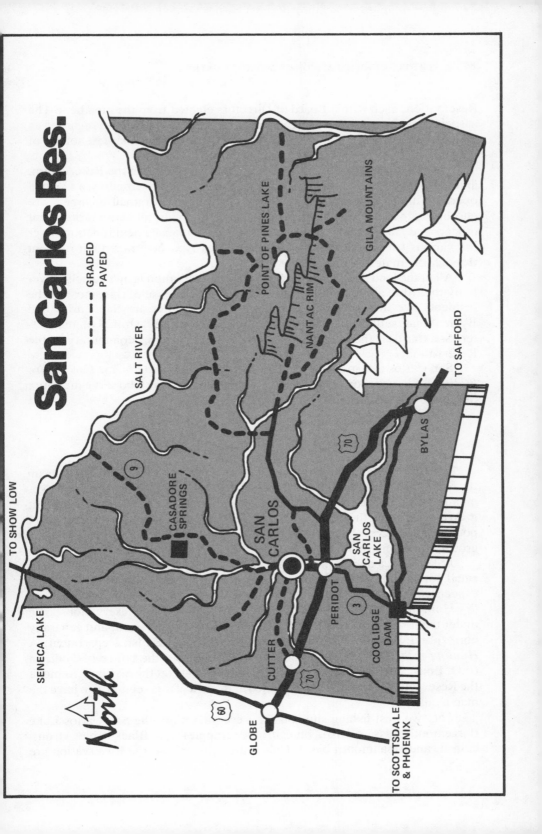

Reservation, each with a Board of Directors elected from the members. The associations raise purebreed, registered Hereford cattle that are regarded as among the best in the U.S.—and provide the tribe with its largest source of income.

There are presently over 7,000 San Carlos Apaches on the Reservation, and the population is growing steadily. The tribe is governed by a Council operating under a written charter and constitution. Council members are chosen by popular elections. The Council appoints all law enforcement officers and judges, and is authorized to exercise management functions over the various tribal enterprises. The San Carlos Apaches trace their descent through the maternal line.

All of the land making up the San Carlos Reservation is owned collectively by the tribe, and individual use is regulated. Because of this, most of the residents live in towns. The two largest communities are San Carlos and Bylas. Small settlements include Peridot, Eight Mile Wash, Calva and Cutter. San Carlos is the tribal headquarters and the principal community on the Reservation.

San Carlos is also home-base for the well-known *Southwest Forest Fire Fighters*, a large group of professional Indian fire-fighters who serve the entire Southwest during the summer "forest fire" months.

Recreational Opportunities

Fishing, camping and hunting are the primary recreational attractions on the San Carlos Reservation, with fishing the most popular. San Carlos Lake, mentioned earlier, the largest lake on the Reservation (and one of the largest in Arizona), holds the Arizona records for catfish (65 pounds) and crappie (4 pounds, 10 ounces). Facilities at the lake include camping and picnic areas, a grocery store, marina, bait and curio shop and mobile home park.

Lake Seneca and Point of Pines Lake, along with many of the dozens of small ponds and streams on the Reservation, are also popular with anglers— especially those who like to get further away from the beaten track.

Hunting and fishing regulations on the San Carlos Reservation come under the jurisdiction of the Tribal Game & Fish Commission, and generally correspond with those of the Arizona State Game & Fish Department. A *Hunting & Fishing Map,* in color, is available from the Office of Tourism (P.O. Box 0, San Carlos, Arizona 85550) for 50 cents (at this writing). Some of the Reservation "permit" dealers listed at the end of this section also have the map available.

The two best fishing sites on the Reservation are the San Carlos Lake (largemouth bass, catfish, bluegill and crappie) and Black River (trout, catfish, and smallmouth bass). Cold water streams on the Reservation are planted with Rainbow, German Brown and other trout species by the Bureau of Sport Fisheries and Wildlife.

Among the big game hunting species available on the Reservation are elk, whitetail deer, mule deer, bear, mountain lion and javelina. Predators include coyotes, fox and bobcats. Small game species include rabbits, squirrel, quail, dove, pigeon, ducks and geese. Wild turkey are also found on the Reservation, but non-Indians are not permitted to hunt either turkey or deer.

Visitors who want to hunt or fish on the San Carlos Reservation must have the appropriate Reservation licenses, tags and permits. Those going after elk, bear, javelina and mountain lion must also have licenses *and tags* from the Arizona State Game & Fish Department. Arizona State permits, by drawing, are required for elk, deer and javelina.

Fishing is permitted all year around on the San Carlos Reservation. Anglers intending to fish only at San Carlos Lake do not need a Reservation fishing permit, but they *do* need a Reservation "access permit." A Reservation fishing permit *is* required for fishing in all other lakes, ponds and streams on the Reservation. (All non-Indian anglers in Arizona are required by state law to have a state fishing license regardless of where they fish.)

Fishermen with permits from the San Carlos Reservation may also fish on the north banks of the Black and Salt Rivers, the boundary line between the San Carlos and Fort Apache Reservations. A San Carlos permit is *not* good for fishing in any other Fort Apache Reservation waters.

San Carlos Campgrounds

Developed campgrounds on the San Carlos Indian Reservation that are open to the public include the San Carlos Marina Resort, Seneca Park, Point of Pines Lake and Cassadore Springs.

The San Carlos Lake Resort complex includes a large coffee shop, a curio-gift and tackle shop, and a trailer-and-camper park with 100 pads equipped with electric, water and sewer hookups. Rates at the trailer/camper park are available by the day, week or month.

Seneca Park, 33 miles north of Globe just off of Highway 60, includes a 27-surface-acre lake that is kept stocked with trout; picnic tables, fireplaces, toilet facilities and drinking water. There is also a restaurant, store and gas station (that are temporarily closed at this writing).

Point of Pine Lakes, some 55 miles from the junction of Route 8 (Geronimo Trail) and Highway 70, has a 35-acre lake with good year-around trout fishing; tables, fireplaces, toilet facilities, drinking water—and numerous other facilities underway. Only 20 miles of the road to the lake are paved; the remainder is "improved trail."

Cassadore Springs, about 10 miles north of San Carlos on Route 9, has spring water, picnic tables, fireplaces, toilets, and shade.

Camping rules and regulations are posted at each campground on the San Carlos Reservation. Campers are reminded that fires are permitted only in prescribed areas, and that only down and dead wood can be burned. All trash is to be placed in containers or pits provided for that purpose; or taken off the Reservation by the camper.

Campgrounds are patrolled by game and fire wardens, and visited regularly by trash-collecting crews (who are *not* responsible for picking up visitors' trash). Campers may select any unoccupied site.

Special Notes

Keep in mind that state permits are required for bandtail pigeon hunting, and that federal waterfowl stamps are required for taking ducks and geese. Only authorized persons may collect waterdogs on the Reservation. Dogs are allowed on the Reservation only with valid state and Reservation permits.

Anyone planning on camping overnight on the San Carlos Reservation— hunter, fisherman or camper—is required to have a camping permit.

Unpaved roads on the San Carlos Reservation are best traveled by pickups and 4-wheel drive vehicles, particularly during the rainy season in and around July; and following snowfalls in the high country in mid-winter. Both San Carlos Lake/Marina Park and Seneca Lake Park are on paved highways, however, and are accessible by passenger cars all year around.

Fishing & Hunting Permit Dealers

CLIFTON
S&S Sporting Goods

GLOBE/MIAMI
A.J. Bayless #62
Globe-Miami Hwy.

A.J. Bayless #63
Box 1493, Globe

Circle K
1250 E. Ash, Globe

Circle K
1951 E. Ash, Globe

Yellow Front Store
1098 N. Broad

Unique Sporting Goods
112 N. Broad St.

PHOENIX/SCOTTSDALE/MESA
Yates Army-Navy Store
4750 N. 16th St., Phoenix

Don's Sport Shop
7801 E. McDowell Rd.
Scottsdale

PIMA
Jerry Taylor Shell Ser.
Box 487, Pima

Zeke's Picnic Supply
Box 205, Central, Az.

PINETOP
Bob Weete's Variety
Box 367

Little Bear's Trading Post

SAFFORD
Talley & Sons
624 8th St.

SAN CARLOS RESERVATION
Bylas Trading Enterprise
Bylas, Az.

Peridot Trading Post
Box 8, Peridot, Az.

San Carlos Lake
Box 0, San Carlos

San Carlos Tribal Business Office
Box 0, San Carlos

TUCSON
F. Ronstadt Hardware
P.O. Box 586

Joe's Eastside Tackle & Bait Shop
5552 E. Speedway

Woody's Sporting Goods Center
1819 N. Stone

Ceremonial Dances

Like their White Mountain neighbors, the San Carlos Apaches still practice a number of traditional Apache ceremonial dances, the most popular of which is the famous Sunrise, or "Puberty," Ceremony.

As detailed in the chapter on the White Mountain Apaches, the purpose of the Sunrise Ceremony is to mark the coming of age of Apache girls, and to entreat the spirits to help them have long, happy lives.

The ceremonials are usually held on weekends during June, July and August in or near San Carlos. To pin down a specific date, call the tribal Tourism Office at 475-2361, ext. 14.

Major Events

The most important annual event on the San Carlos Apache Indian Reservation is the tribal rodeo and fair, held over Veteran's Day weekend in October at San Carlos, the tribal headquarters. One or more ceremonial dances are usually staged during the fair.

Peridot Jewelry

Another visitor-oriented enterprise on the San Carlos Reservation is the mining of peridot, and the manufacturing of peridot jewelry. Peridot is a beautiful, yellowish-green chrysolite (also called olivine), long famous as a gem-stone.

This enterprise is headquartered near the small community of Peridot, at the junction of Highway 70 and 170, between Globe and San Carlos; and appropriately enough is called the Peridot Mining & Manufacturing Enterprise.

The factory is in a large red building (that was once used as a "Skill Center"), a few minutes east of the Globe Municipal Airport. If you are going east toward Peridot and San Carlos, the turn-off is to the left. Proceed on around behind a complex of other buildings. Visitors are welcome at the factory, and may buy peridot jewlery there at wholesale prices.

CAMP VERDE RESERVATION

In the spectacularly beautiful Verde River Valley between Phoenix and Flagstaff—85 miles north of Phoenix; about 50 miles south of Flagstaff—the *Camp Verde Indian Reservation* is home-base for nearly 400 Yavapai and Apache Indians, most of whom live in the communities of Middle Verde, Clarkdale, Camp Verde and Rimrock.

The Reservation is small—only 640 acres. Residents engage in farming, cattle-raising and factory work in a garment factory at Cottonwood. Reservation headquarters is at Camp Verde, just east of the Phoenix-Flagstaff Highway (Interstate 17).

There are several nationally famous Indian ruins in the vicinity (Montezuma Castle National Monument, Tuzigoot National Monument and Montezuma Well; along with the popular Oak Creek Canyon), but none of them are on the Reservation.

YAVAPAI-PRESCOTT RESERVATION

The 1409-acre *Yavapai-Prescott Indian Reservation,* adjoining mile-high Prescott, 96 miles northwest of Phoenix, has fewer than 100 residents. The Yavapais who make their home there are engaged in a long-range program to make the most of their limited size and urban location by encouraging commercial and business development of the property.

FOUR

Central Desert & River Reservations

GILA RIVER INDIAN RESERVATION

The first Indian reservation to be established in Arizona, on February 28, 1859, was the 371,933-acre *Gila River Indian Reservation,* which begins some 15 miles south of present-day Phoenix, extends southward and eastward for several miles, and is home for approximately 9,000 Pima and Maricopa Indians.

The People

The Pimas trace their ancestry to the Hohokam, the legendary civilization that flourished in the Phoenix-Scottsdale area from as early as 300 B.C. to 1500 A.D., and developed a sophisticated canal-irrigation system that was adopted and enlarged by pioneer white Americans when they arrived on the scene in the 1860s and 70s.

The Maricopa neighbors of the Pimas originally lived south of Parker, Arizona along the Colorado River, eventually migrating up the Gila River into central Arizona to avoid confrontations with the Mohaves to the north and the Yumans to the south.

When the famous Jesuit explorer-priest Father Eusebio Kino first visited the land of the Pimas and Maricopas in 1694, he found them flourishing in numerous villages along the banks of the Gila River.

The Pimas and Maricopas were both peaceful and industrious. Their culture was at its peak when white Americans began arriving in Arizona, and they supplied travelers, settlers and U.S. army units with grain and livestock.

Shortly before 1900, however, the waters of the Gila River were dammed up and diverted away from the Reservation. The crops of the Pimas and Maricopas withered, and their fields returned to the desert. They declined into abject poverty. In 1921 about one-fourth of the Gila River Reservation was allotted to individual Indian families. Since then these allotments have been divided and divided again among the descendants of the recipients.

Recovery and Revenge

For well over 100 years the tide of the times went against the Pimas and the Maricopas, bringing them immeasureable suffering and degradation. But as with other Arizona Indians, the pendulum has reversed itself and is now moving in their favor. Because of its location between Metropolitan Phoenix and the communities of Chandler, Casa Grande and Tucson to the south—in the so-called "Golden Corridor"—the wasteland of the Reservation is rapidly becoming some of the most valuable property in the state.

Residents of the Gila River Reservation now engage in a variety of on and off-Reservation activities, including farming, diamond-cutting and polishing, cattle-raising, sugar processing, industrial manufacturing, computer card key-punching, and the production of traditional handicrafts.

With their eyes on the future, the Pimas and Maricopas have developed an overall land-use plan for the entire reservation, with emphasis on recreational and cultural centers and industrial parks. Three of the latter—the Pima-Coolidge Industrial Park, three miles north of Coolidge; the Pima-Chandler Industrial Park, 15 miles south of Phoenix; and the San Tan Industrial Park, 35 miles south of Phoenix—are already well underway.

Most of the Reservation residents live in or near the communities of Sacaton and San Tan. Sacaton is the largest community on the Reservation, and is headquarters for the tribal government.

Visitor Attractions

There are presently four major visitor attractions on the Gila River Reservation—The *Gila River Arts & Crafts Center,* the *Firebird Lake Water Sports World, Mul-Cha-Tha* ("The Gathering of the People"), and the annual *St. Johns Mission School Fair.*

About 30 minutes south of Phoenix and Scottsdale, just off the Phoenix-Tucson Freeway (Interstate 10), the *Gila River Arts & Crafts Center* includes a museum, a large and attractive handicraft gift shop featuring an Indian jewelry room, pottery rooms, baskets, rugs, kachina dolls and other crafts;

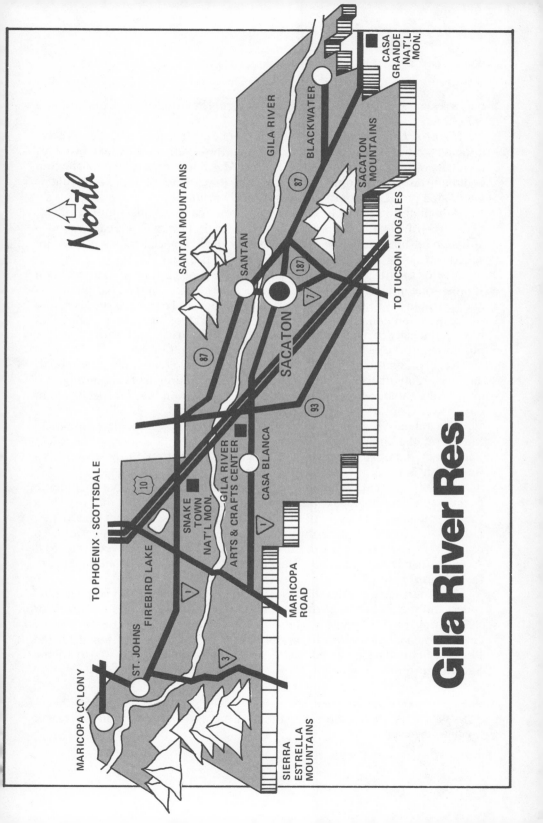

Gila River Res.

plus a restaurant. The strikingly designed complex is open daily from 9 a.m. to 5:30 p.m.

Firebird Lake Water Sports World is one of the most ambitious recreational facilities on any of Arizona's Indian Reservations. The lake provides residents of Phoenix, Scottsdale, Tempe, Mesa and other Valley of the Sun communities with the opportunity to go boating, water-skiing, swimming or water-side picnicking only minutes from their homes.

Adjoining Interstate 10 Freeway at Maricopa Road, just south of Phoenix, Firebird Lake is open daily from 7 a.m. to 11 p.m. the year around— although all boats must be off the lake by dusk. Special racing events are scheduled at the lake at various times during the year.

Visitor facilities at Firebird Lake include a restaurant, two concession stands—one in the swimming beach area and the other in the boat-pit area— and restrooms. Visitors may bring their own food and beverage supplies onto the reservation complex, with the exception of alcoholic drinks. Beer, that has been legally brought onto the Reservation by tribal authorities, may be purchased at the restaurant and concession stands, however.

Regular admittance fees at Firebird Lake include four categories: a boat- and-driver; all others 12 years of age and older; children from six through 11; and children under six. The latter are free. Admission fees on special-event days vary. Call 963-2962 for current prices.

The annual *St. John's Indian Fair* is usually held on the first Sunday in March, at the Indian mission school in Komatke, 17 miles southwest of Phoenix on the western end of the Gila River Reservation. Purpose of the all- Indian fair is to raise funds for the school.

A popular event attended by thousands, the fair attractions include an Indian-style beef barbecue, an Indian handicrafts bazaar, and midway rides for the youngsters. The school's famous Indian dancers, made up of students, put on several performances during the day. Activity begins around 9 a.m. To reach from the Phoenix area, drive west on Van Buren Avenue to 51st Avenue, turn left (south) and follow the signs. It is 17 miles from Phoenix to the mission.

The fourth major attraction on the Gila River Reservation is the annual rodeo and fair at Sacaton, tribal headquarters, known as *Mul-Cha-Tha,* or "Gathering of the People." Held in late January or early February, the celebration includes arts and crafts exhibits. To reach Sacaton from the Phoenix-Scottsdale area, go south on the Tucson Freeway (I-10) to the Sacaton turn-off.

---

*The 1976 *Mul-Cha-Tha* was cancelled, and as of this writing there are no plans to continue the event.

FT. MCDOWELL RESERVATION

About 15 miles northeast of the Phoenix-Scottsdale area, along the banks of the picturesque Verde River, the *Ft. McDowell Indian Reservation* was created on September 15, 1903 for groups of Mohave, Yavapai and Apache Indians who had long lived in the area. The name of the Reservation was taken from the famous territorial military fort that occupied a commanding point just above the river.

The Reservation consists of 24,680 acres of low desert hills and tree-covered river bottom-lands. Some 350 residents engage in farming, cattle-raising, gravel mining, and wood-cutting. The plush, planned community of *Fountain Hills* adjoins the Reservation on the northwest.

A dam proposed for construction in the vicinity of the conflux of the Verde and Salt Rivers, some three miles to the south, would inundate most of the usable area of the Reservation beneath a large lake.

The Weather

The Ft. McDowell Reservation is only 300 or so feet higher than Phoenix and Scottsdale (which are about 1100 feet above sea-level), but being closer to massive mountain ranges, the Reservation has a slightly cooler summer climate than the Valley of the Sun communities, and gets more rain.

Afternoon temperatures in July average around 105 degrees; in January about 66 degrees. At the village of McDowell, where tribal headquarters is located, there is an average of 9.22 inches of rain each year, and an inch of snow (none of the latter in Phoenix, Scottsdale, Mesa, etc.).

Visitor Attractions

Only visitor attraction on the Reservation is the Verde River, which is lined with slightly improved and unimproved picnic and camping sites, and draws thousands of heat-flushed Valleyites during the summer months.

Besides picnicking, camping, swimming (in the deeper pools) and hiking, the Reservation portion of the Verde is also a popular "inner-tube float run." Some tubing enthusiasts go into the water at the Highway 87 bridge. Others begin their float two or three miles further up-river.

Ft. McDowell village is the only community on the Reservation. It is located a short distance north of Highway 87 via Ft. McDowell Rd. It is *not* a tourist attraction.

The most accessible area of the Verde River is the west bank, via dirt roads and unimproved "trails" branching off from Ft. McDowell Road, which parallels the river only a few hundred yards away. Some of these access roads, especially those on the south side of Highway 87, are little more than ruts through the underbrush, and pass through patches of soft sand. Passenger cars that stop in soft areas frequently get stuck and have to be pulled out.

The only riverside facilities are a few concrete tables, benches and trash barrels. Some of the tables have been upset by shifting sands during past spring floods. Anyone planning on camping in the area in the early summer months should bring along mosquito repellent in addition to the other supplies you need to be self-sufficient. (There is a tribal grocery store at the intersection of Highway 87 and Ft. McDowell Rd.)

During the summer months, tribal rangers sometimes man booths alongside of Ft. McDowell Road to collect nominal "recreational use" fees from visitors heading for the river. The rangers may also drive around the picnic and camping areas, collecting on-the-spot.

SALT RIVER INDIAN RESERVATION

The *Salt River Indian Reservation,* created on June 14, 1879, adjoins Scottsdale on the west, Mesa on the south and the Ft. McDowell Reservation on the north. The 49,294-acre Reservation, with a population of approximately 3,000 Pima and Maricopa Indians, sets astride the Salt River, and takes in the conflux of the Salt and Verde Rivers, about 30 miles east of Phoenix.

There are two communities on the reservation—Salt River, the tribal headquarters, located at 10,000 East McDowell Road (the same McDowell Rd. that goes through Phoenix and Scottsdale); and Lehi, about three miles further east on the north side of Salt River.

Economic activities on the Reservation include farming, cattle and horse-raising, land-leasing, and several annual visitor-oriented spectator-recreational events that attract thousands.

Visitor Attractions

The two major annual events on the Salt River Indian Reservation are the *All-Indian Arts & Crafts Christmas Bazaar,* held in early December, and the *Salt River Indian Trade Fair,* held the last weekend in March.

The 3-day All-Indian Arts & Crafts Christmas Bazaar, located in the Pi-Copa Gym in the village of Salt River, features arts and crafts made by Indians from Arizona, New Mexico, California, Idaho and sometimes other Western states.

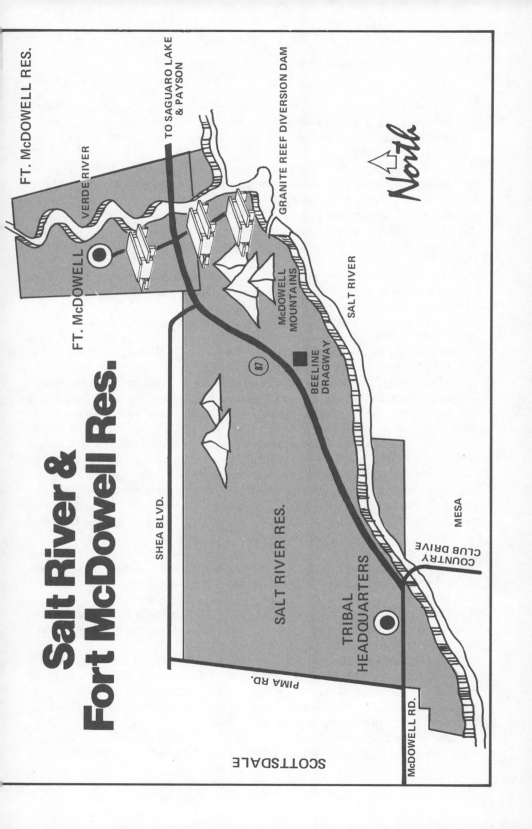

Salt River & Fort McDowell Res.

FT. McDOWELL RES.

FT. McDOWELL

TO SAGUARO LAKE & PAYSON

VERDE RIVER

GRANITE REEF DIVERSION DAM

McDOWELL MOUNTAINS

SALT RIVER

87

BEELINE DRAGWAY

North

SHEA BLVD.

SALT RIVER RES.

TRIBAL HEADQUARTERS

MESA

COUNTRY CLUB DRIVE

PIMA RD.

McDOWELL RD.

SCOTTSDALE

The bazaar is strictly Indian—sponsored and managed by Indians, with Indians operating the booths. All of the items offered for sale—baskets, rugs, jewelry, leather-wear, pottery, etc.—are guaranteed in both quality and origin.

The Friday-through-Sunday sales show begins each day at 8 a.m. Food booths, serving traditional dishes from several tribes, are available for those who want to make a day of it.

The Salt River Indian Trade Fair in late March is more or less a repeat of the All-Indian bazaar in December, but tends to have more exhibitors, some of them coming from as far as Alaska and the Sierra Madre Mountains in Mexico.

The trade fair, staged on the grounds outside Pi-Copa Gym at Salt River, has been expanding each year. Its sponsors say their goal is to make it a truly all American Indian happening.

For exact dates of the two events, contact the Mesa Chamber of Commerce (tel. 969-1307), the Scottsdale Chamber of Commerce (tel. 945-8481), or write to the Indian sponsors, c/o Rt. 1, Box 356, Scottsdale, Arizona 85256 —in late November or mid-March.

Other Reservation events of special interest to visitors: the annual January-thru-March basketball tournaments featuring Indian players from around the state; the *Annual Southwest All-Indian Women's Softball Tournament* in mid-August; the *Annual Red Mountain Classic All-Indian Men's Softball Tournament,* also in August; and the *All-Indian Southwest Baseball Tournament,* held in late August— all at the Pi-Copa Gym in Salt River.

The most important visitor recreation attraction on the Salt River Reservation is the river itself, with its shoreline camping and picnic grounds. To reach the Reservation's *Salt River Recreation Area* from Phoenix-Scottsdale, go east on Highway 87 to Ft. McDowell Road, just before the highway crosses the Verde River. Turn right onto the narrow paved road and proceed south for about three miles or until you reach the river area. Any of the unimproved turn-offs to the left of the narrow road will take you to the Verde River just a few hundred feet away (at this point still on the Ft. McDowell Reservation).

There are some tables and barbecue pits in the Salt River Recreation Area, but no other facilities. Reservation rangers may come around and collect a small fee for the use of the area.

The Salt, a larger (and cooler!) river than the Verde, which merges into it just above the low Granite Reef Dam, is also the most popular as a "tubing river." The more ambitious "floaters" start their down-stream journey just below Saguaro Lake several miles to the north, and end up on the Reservation, usually at Blue Point Bridge.

There are a number of facilities on the Salt River Reservation that are operated by non-Indian commercial enterprises. These include the *Bee Line*

Speedway auto racing course adjoining Bee Line Highway east of the tribal headquarters; a trap-shoot range; the beautiful *Roadrunner Golf Course,* the elaborate *Roadrunner Travel Trailer Park,* and *Speilman-Ford Mobile Home Park.*

Dates and Times

For current dates and times of the annual events on the Reservation, call the tribal Recreation Department at 833-4842.

FIVE

Southern Arizona Reservations

PAPAGO LAND

The 3-part *Papago Indian Reservation,* covering a total of 2,854,789 acres, is the second largest reservation in Arizona. The main part of the Reservation stretches some 90 miles across south-central Arizona, shares a common border on the south with Mexico, and is 2,773,357 acres big. The two other parts of the Reservation are the *San Xavier District* (71,095 acres) just south of Tucson, and the *Gila Bend Reservation* (10,337 acres), immediately north of the town by that name, 60 miles southwest of Phoenix. The San Xavier portion of the Reservation was established on July 1, 1874; the primary portion on December 12, 1882.

The main part of Papago Land consists of great expanses of desert plains and valleys, broken here and there by hills and mountain ranges that jut up on the horizon like islands at sea. Elevation on the Reservation goes from a desert low of 2,674 feet to Baboquivari Peak, which soars to a magnificent 7,730 feet from the surrounding plains.

The second most conspicuous geographic feature on the Papago Reservation is another towering peak—the famous Kitt Peak, which at 6,875 feet is the highest point in the Quinlan Mountain Range. The typical vista in Papago Land is therefore one of immense distances, with hills and mountain ranges in the foreground (or background!), and these two pinnacles—regarded by the Papago as the homes of their ancient gods and thus sacred—keeping silent vigil over all. From many points on the Reservation, the great white tower of the internationally famed observatory on Kitt Peak can be seen from up to 40 miles away.

On the east, the Papago Reservation border follows the crest of the massive Baboquivari Mountain Range. On the west it adjoins the 300,000-

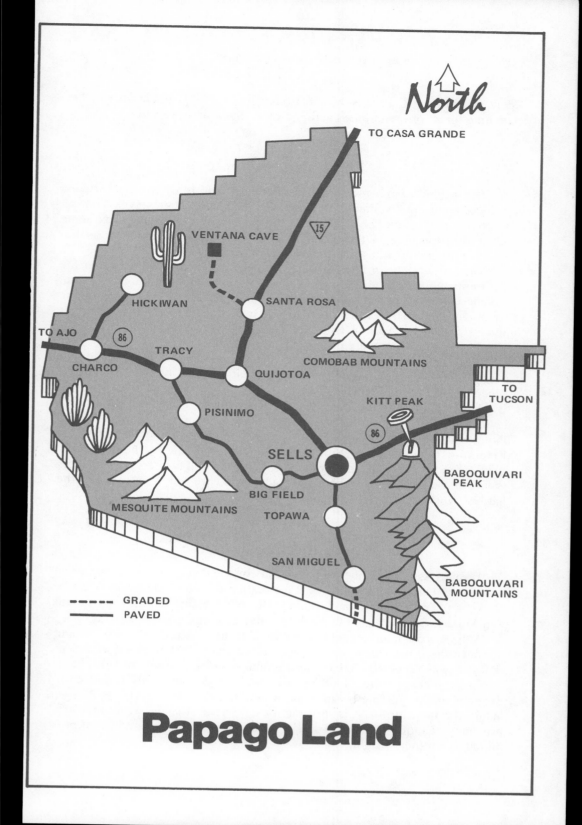

Papago Land

acre *Organ Pipe Cactus National Monument,* which is made up of a fascinating forest of organ pipe cacti and other Sonoran desert life.

The Papago People

The name *Papago* means "Bean People," and is what other Arizona Indians traditionally called the Papago. They call themselves *Tohono Awawtam* or "Desert People." Today there are close to 7,000 Papagos, some 3,000 of whom live in the town of Sells, the largest community on the Reservation and administrative headquarters for the tribe.

The pre-white-man Papago were a remarkable people, with one of the most enlightened moralities ever devised by man. They did not believe in violence, and did not make war against the Spanish, the Mexicans or the Americans. When they were forced to fight to defend their homes and families against forays by Apache and Yavapai raiders, however, they were formidable warriors and were usually the victors.

When an individual Papago had to kill another human being, even in self-defense, he had to undergo a 16-day purification ritual before he could be accepted back into his own society!

The Papago were farmers when the Spanish arrived; working their own lands when there was enough moisture to bring in crops, and hiring out to the Pimas and Maricopas—whose farms were watered by the Salt and Gila Rivers—in other seasons. With the introduction of cattle by the Spaniards, the Papago also became cattle ranchers. They are still farmers and ranchers today, as well as copper miners and traders, and are widely regarded as the hardest working of Arizona's Indians.

Where the Papago Live

Besides Sells, the principal community on the Papago Reservation, there are over a dozen small to tiny villages scattered around, including Charco, Hickiwan, Tracy, Quijotoa, Pisinimo, Big Field, Santa Rosa, Topawa and San Miguel. Some Papago families also live in remote outlying areas.

Sells was originally called *Indian Oasis* because the presence of water and a village there had made it a favorite stop-over for travelers since ancient times. It was renamed after Indian Commissioner Cato Sells in 1918.

Sixty miles southwest of Tucson on Highway 86, Sells is presently experiencing a building boom in both new housing and service buildings. While the townsite itself is in a picturesque area—the desert around it is pristinely beautiful—Sells is a singularly unimpressive town and is not promoted as a "tourist sight."

The Weather

The lower desert regions of the Papago Indian Reservation get from five to eight inches of rainfall a year, and have a typical desert climate—scorching hot summers, brief periods of almost perfect weather in the early spring and late fall (mild days and cool nights), and warm-to-cool days and cold night during the mid-winter months. Of course, the higher the altitude the cooler the temperatures and the more precipitation. Above the 5,000-foot level in its mountain ranges, the Reservation has an alpine climate, including winter snows.

Mid-summer travelers crossing the Reservation do not usually tarry long at desert-level (and should be exceedingly wary about venturing off of paved roads into unknown areas if they are not experienced with—and prepared for —the dehydrating heat of the desert sun). By the same token, the mild winters make the colorful Papago desert seem like a kind of paradise during that season.

Attractions in Papago Land

There are two major visitor attractions on the Papago Indian Reservation: *Kitt Peak National Observatory,* and the annual *Papago Tribal Fair and Rodeo* at Sells. Minor attractions include Ventana Cave (inhabited as early as 20,000 years ago), Forteleza Ruins, and the Vaivo Vo Water Reservation Area, which centers around the lake formed by Jackrabbit Dam.

Kitt Peak National Observatory—Every year over half a million people, from all over the U.S. and other countries around the world, take the easy and scenic drive to the top of towering Kitt Peak to see the largest complex of astronomical instruments in the world, and learn something about what "The people with the long eyes" do.

Established in 1958 after long negotiations to convince the Papagos that neither the astronomers nor their telescopes would desecrate the sacred peak, the complex sets in the center of a 200-acre site surrounded by tall pines and craggy peaks, with a view of the surrounding desert that is uplifting to say the least.

The most impressive of the observatory's 14 telescopes is the Robert R. McMath Solar Telescope, built for observation of the sun, and the largest of its kind in the world. The tracking lens rest on top of a 110-foot tower (visible for miles from the vast desert below). The images it gathers are reflected down a 500-foot track, the last 300 feet of which is through a shaft cored into the mountain.

The extraordinary complex, owned by the National Science Foundation and operated in collaboration with several universities, includes a Visitor's Center and Museum. Just below the observatory is a picnic area maintained for visitors. It has indoor flush toilets, drinking water, tables and barbecue fireplaces. The peak and its facilities are open to the public from 10 a.m. to 4 p.m. daily, with guided tours twice a day on weekends and holidays.

All-Indian Papago Tribal Fair & Rodeo—This is the biggest event on the Reservation, and is usually held on the third weekend in November each year. A *Miss Papago Contest* is held in conjunction with the fair. Besides the rodeo action, visitors have a chance to shop for Papago-made baskets and other handicrafts, try Indian food, and see lots of Indians. To confirm the date of the fair, call the tribal office in Sells, tel. 383-2221; or the Tucson Chamber of Commerce, tel. 792-1212.

Ventana Cave, for those with an archaeology-bent, is located near the village of Gu Achi in the Santa Rosa Valley, off Highway 15 between Quijotoa and Casa Grande.

Camping Notes

There are several areas where visitors can camp on the Papago Indian Reservation. Those with facilities include the Kitt Peak grounds and Baboquivari Canyon (see map). Camping permits are required and have to be obtained directly from the office of the tribal treasurer in Sells, since there are no tourist or recreation offices on the Reservation.

Tribal offices in Sells are located some distance to the south of Highway 86 (several hundred yards), via a paved side-road.

THE SAN XAVIER RESERVATION DISTRICT

The *San Xavier Indian Reservation*, about 15 minutes south of Tucson via the Nogales Freeway, is the site of one of Arizona's most famous visitor attractions—*Mission San Xavier del Bac*, or the "White Dove of the Desert."

Visible from the highway several miles before you reach the turn-off, the famous mission was originally founded in 1700. The present building was begun in 1783 and completed in 1797. It is regarded as the most beautiful example of mission architecture in the American Southwest. It is open to the public from 9 a.m. to 6 p.m. daily except Sundays.

The mission is still in daily use by the Indian residents of the Reservation. Its major "public" event is the annual *San Xavier Fiesta* on the first Friday after Easter, commemorating the founding of the mission.

The Fiesta, produced by the Tucson Festival Society, consists of a spectacular torch-lit procession of some 400 to 500 Papago and Yaqui Indians, overhead fireworks and tolling bells. The procession itself begins at 8 p.m. (and lasts about an hour), but dance groups of Indian children begin performing about 6 p.m.

Crowds gather for the festival as early as 5 p.m., to "stake out" good viewing spots (there are no seats of any kind, so visitors who want to sit down must bring their own portable chairs).

A special feature of the annual program are the food-booths set up and manned by Papago women, serving "barbecue plates" consisting of meat, beans, salad and a choice of other traditional Indian corn/meat dishes.

The Gila Bend District

There are no visitor attractions or facilities on the *Gila Bend District* of the Papago Indian Reservation.

AK CHIN RESERVATION

Thirty miles south of Phoenix in the now very dry Santa Cruz River Valley, the *Ak Chin Indian Reservation* has approximately 300 Papago residents whose major activity is operating Ak Chin Farms. There is also some livestock feeding on the Reservation.

The Reservation is fairly large—21,840 acres—but is primarily arid desert; its potential now limited by lack of water. The residents are the descendents of Papagos who lived along the banks of the once free-flowing Santa Cruz River for generations. The river was bottled up by Coolidge Dam in 1929.

SIX

Western Arizona Reservations

THE COLORADO RIVER RESERVATION

Some 1600 members of the Mohave, Chemehuevi, Hopi and Apache tribes share this river-centered Reservation, which is made up of 225,995 acres in Arizona and 42,969 additional acres across the Colorado River in California. Established on March 3, 1865, the *Colorado River Indian Reservation* was the second Reservation to be set up in Arizona.

The Reservation fronts on both sides of the Colorado River, giving it 90 miles of shore-line, and a major resource of inestimable value. The geography of the Reservation ranges from river bottomlands, bluffs, rolling hills and narrow, flat-bottom valleys, to rather broad plains sloping river-ward.

The Colorado River People

The Mohave and Chemehuevi residents of the Reservation are truly "river people." The few Hopi and Apache families who live among them originally came from the plateaus of northern Arizona and mountains in the eastern sector of the state (See the Apache and Hopi chapters).

The Mohave, members of the Yuma-speaking tribes, have lived along the Colorado River for centuries, farming the bottomlands and reaping other sustenance from the wildlife and natural plants in the area. Traditionally ruled over by hereditary chiefs, their early social life revolved around ceremonial dances and long wakes preceding cremation of the dead.

In summer the Mohaves lived in homes made of willow and cottonwood branches plastered with mud; their winter homes were partly underground, "pit-style," or dug back into banks. The Mohave were known for their finely beaded collars, belts, necklaces, and pottery. Other handicrafts included

Colorado River Res.

North

BLYTHE

CALIFORNIA

POSTON

PARKER

EARP

LAKE MOOVALYA

TO LAKE HAVASU CITY

"11 MILE PARKER STRIP"

95

72

TO PHOENIX

TO PHOENIX

10 95

dolls, gourd rattlers and colorfully decorated cradleboards. Today the best of the Mohave crafts are sold through the tribal museum gift shop in Parker.

The Chemehuevi were originally Southern Paiutes who roamed up and down the Colorado River from Nevada to Yuma, without fixed, permanent homes. They were hunters and gatherers, and lived a primitive existence. They were, however, master basket weavers, using willow and cottonwood, decorated with dynamic designs made from black devil's claw fibers or juncus, a brown or yellow marsh reed.

In the early Territorial days of Arizona, there were numerous clashes between the Chemehuevi and Mohave, but the two tribes have long since "buried the hatchet," and share the same Reservation peacefully.

The Weather

The weather on the Colorado River Reservation is very predictable—hot and dry in the summer, and very warm to cool in the winter. It is frequently the hottest spot in the state in mid-summer, and vies with Yuma for being the warmest in winter. Some 11 months out of the year, the skies are a burnished blue, matched only by the blue of the placid (in this area!) Colorado River.

The average daytime high in January is 67.1 degrees F., with night-time lows averaging 33.1 during the same month. There is an occasional trace of snow on rare overcast and cold winter days, and less than five inches of rain the year around.

In July, the hottest month, the daytime temperatures soar to 108 and higher, but it cools to an average of 76.2 degrees at night. And there is always the cool, inviting Colorado.

The area is a favorite wintering place for retirees, and a mecca for recreation seekers of all ages all year around.

Where the People Live

Principal communities on the Colorado River Reservation are Parker and Poston in Arizona, and Blythe and Earp in California. A number of families also live in outlying areas on farms.

Farming (mostly on irrigated lands), tourism, trade and manufacturing give the residents of the Reservation a relatively high standard of living.

Visitor Attractions

The major visitor attraction on the Reservation is the beautiful Colorado River, which runs deep and serene in this area because of a series of dams that gentle the raging torrent rushing out of the Grand Canyon further up. These dams—Headgate which forms Moovalya Lake, and Parker, which forms Lake Havasu—make this long stretch of the Colorado River one of the major inland water recreational areas in the Southwest.

Recreational Facilities

Both banks of the Reservation's Colorado River frontage have been turned into a resort/recreational land from Parker to a point some 11 miles up-river. Within this so-called "11-Mile Parker Strip," there are resort motels, trailer parks, campgrounds, picnic sites, marinas, and boat slips by the score. There are some 30 motels in the immediate area of Parker alone.

The Blue Water Marina, a tribal enterprise on Blue Water Lagoon, has cabanas, a restaurant, its own private beach, and a trailer park.

Annual Events

There are several annual events on the Colorado River Reservation that attract thousands of spectators and participants. These include:

Annual International Inner-Tube Race—This is an inner-tube river float that begins in Blue Water Lagoon—on or about June 21—and ends seven miles downstream at Big River Park, on the California side.

There are age categories for "racers" who want to compete for cash prizes and for fame, and a good time for those who join in just for fun. Tubers who want to participate in the contest portion of the day's festivities sign up at the Blue Water Marina.

Southern California Speedboat Inboard Regattas—Twice a year, in May and on Thanksgiving Day, the Southern California Speedboat Club of Los Angeles sponsors speedboat regattas and numerous other boat races, including outboard, jet, boat-and-water-ski drag races, at Blue Water Lagoon. The races—and other recreational opportunities in general—attract masses of people to the Reservation on these occasions.

Parker 9-Hour Enduro—Held on the first Sunday in March (when it is bikini weather by 10 a.m.), the Parker 9-Hour Enduro is a one-of-a-kind spectacle. Eighty of the largest and fastest boats in the world put on a racing marathon that draws 30–40,000 spectators.

All-Indian Rodeo—An early December activity, this annual affair attracts Indian cowboys from all over Arizona and the West. It is held at the Parker rodeo grounds.

Indian Day Celebration—Part of *National Indian Day,* this late September weekend celebration includes a parade, two barbecues, an arts and crafts show, Indian dancing, a Miss Colorado Indian Pageant and lots of general merrymaking. To pin down current year dates and times, call tribal head-quarters at (602) 669-9211.

Fishing & Hunting

The Reservation portion of the Colorado River is a fisherman's paradise, and attracts anglers—especially in the winter—from as far away as Canada. Dove, quail, water fowl and rabbits thrive in the vicinity of the river, and also attract hunters from all over. There are deer on the reservation, but non-Indians are not allowed to hunt them.

Fishing and hunting permits may be purchased from the tribal administrative office in Parker, from tribal game officers, and from several sporting goods shops in Parker.

Shopper Notes

Handicrafts made by Colorado River Indians and others are on sale at the Colorado River Indian Museum gift shop on Mohave Road and 2nd Avenue, 1 mile southwest of Parker, and at King's Thunderbird Lodge and Winner's Circle, both on Riverside Drive in Parker.

When in Poston, check to see if the Senior Citizens' Clock Factor is open. When in operation, Hopi, Mohave, Chemehuevi and Navajo craftsmen make beautiful mosaic clocks of brilliantly colored sands.

COCOPAH RESERVATION

Sixteen miles south of Yuma, and divided into two sections, East Cocopah and West Cocopah, this 598-acre Reservation is virtually all agricultural. Most of the approximately 300 tribal members are farmers. A few work off-Reservation. Tribal headquarters is on West Cocopah.

The major Indian Reservation attraction in the Yuma area is the infamous *Ft. Yuma Territorial Prison,* just across the Colorado River from Yuma on the California side, on the Ft. Yuma Indian Reservation. Part of the prison, which housed some of the most notorious desperadoes of the Old West, has been turned into a museum. Facilities include a gift shop and restaurant. Open daily except Christmas.

SEVEN

Evaluating & Buying Indian Jewelry

Jewelry made by Arizona (and New Mexico) Indians is one of the most distinctive and popular "Indian art forms" still flourishing in the U.S. The hand-made products of the most skilled and famous Indian artisans become collectors' items, with their value spiraling upwards, the moment they are sold.

The Spanish introduced silversmithing to the Zuni Indians of New Mexico in the late 1500s. Arizona's Hopi Indians learned it from the Zuni. The Navajo learned the art from Mexican artists in the 1800s. Today in Arizona only the Hopi and Navajo create silver—and silver-turquoise—jewelry.

There are two categories of Indian silver and silver-turquoise jewelry—hand-made and machine-made. Only hand-made Indian jewelry is regarded as "authentic" by many; and because of the additional time required to produce it, hand-made items are generally more expensive than machine-made versions.

Most hand-made Indian jewelry can be distinguished from the machine-made because of its "rough" hand-beaten finish. The artist may also put his name or initials on the back of the work. Reliable dealers will also tell prospective customers which is hand-made and which is machine-made.

Jewelry is particularly important to the Navajo and Hopi, who wear it not only for its decorative effect but also as a measure of their economic well-being. Many of the "contemporary" jewelry designs produced by Navajo and Hopi craftsmen are ancient; taken from pottery shards that are hundreds of years old.

Before the Reservation visitor, or shopper at an off-Reservation Indian trading post, can properly evaluate Indian-made jewelry, it is necessary to know something about its materials—silver and turquoise. The following is provided as an abbreviated guide to evaluating and buying Indian-made jewelry:

109

Turquoise is a semi-precious stone so far found in only a few places in the world—China, Iran, Russia, and in the American states of Colorado, New Mexico, Nevada and Arizona. It is not a primary metal, and is always found in veins of other stone. Scientifically speaking, it is a "hydrous aluminum phosphate colored by copper salts." The markings on turquoise, known as its "matrix," are caused by other rock.

The color of turquoise ranges from pale blue to dark green. The blue is from its copper content; the green from the iron it contains. The quality of turquoise is determined by the intensity and depth of its color, its hardness and the attractiveness of its matrix.

Dealers sometimes identify turquoise by association with its place of origin. *Bisbee Blue* is a bright, almost royal blue turquoise—without a matrix—mined at Bisbee, Arizona. *Morenci Blue* is a lighter blue with a dark matrix. Turquoise mined in Globe, Arizona is light blue with a lighter matrix than that of Morenci. Kingman turquoise has a green hue and is veined with more and finer matrixes.

Turquoise is often combined with silver in a technique called *inlaying,* developed by the Zuni of New Mexico, and now also used by the Hopi of Arizona. This is a technique of setting turquoise in silver, or mounting it on silver.

"Silver" terms that you need to know include two kinds of silver—"German silver," which is an alloy of copper, zinc and nickel, and is not used by Arizona Indians; and "Indian" silver, or silver that is almost pure, with 925 parts silver and 75 parts copper. There are two silversmithing processes you should be familiar with: "sandcasting" and "overlaying."

Sandcasting is a method of making silver into jewelry by melting it and pouring it into a mould. The resulting piece is very rough and must be filed and polished. Bracelets are cast flat and shaped by hammering. Sandcasting is used primarily by the Navajo, although some Hopi craftsmen use the technique.

Overlaying refers to using two sheets of silver. A design is cut into one of the sheets. It is then heated and soldered to the second sheet. The bottom sheet is darkened with a sulphur mix to emphasize the design. This technique is favored by the Hopi.

It is regarded as legitimate to harden turquoise by exposing it to pressure, and to color it by dyeing. While turquoise treated in this matter will last longer than an untreated piece, it is considered less valuable by connoisseurs. Untreated, soft turquoise will change color over a period of time, from contact with the body.

One of the most popular pieces of Arizona Indian jewelry is the "squash blossom." This is a necklace of silver beads with many silver "blossoms" hanging from them. At the center of the necklace is a *naja;* a crescent-shaped silver pendant that may be inlaid with turquoise.

Your best safeguards are to buy your Indian jewelry from an Indian tribal shop when you are on a Reservation, and to go to an established, reputable dealer who specializes in such jewelry when you are shopping off-Reservation.

There are many long-established and well-known off-Reservation Indian jewelry shops in Phoenix, Scottsdale, Tucson, Flagstaff and other Arizona communities—including complete Indian arts and crafts trading posts. One of the oldest and best-known Indian jewelry dealers is the Fred Harvey chain, which has some 40 retail stores of its own, and also wholesales Indian jewelry to other dealers throughout the country.

Annual Off-Reservation
Indian Events in Arizona

Several of Arizona's largest and most important "Indian Events"—along with some that are small-scale but of special interest—are off-Reservation, and involve the local non-Indian communities as sponsors or participants, or both. Among those that are regularly scheduled:

JANUARY–AUGUST

Tri-West Indian Arts & Crafts Show & Sales— Each year Tri-West Enterprises Inc. of Phoenix stages five Indian arts and craft shows-and-sales that are said to be the largest of their type in the country. The first show of the year is in Tucson at the *Tucson Community Center,* usually over the second weekend in January. The second show is in Phoenix at the *Civic Plaza Center,* in late March and/or early April. The third show of the year is at the *Anaheim Convention Center* in Anaheim, California in late July-early-August. The fourth show, held in Los Angeles at the *L.A. Convention Center,* is usually over the first weekend in August. The fifth and final show of the year is at the *San Francisco Cow Palace,* in mid-August.

The Tri-West Indian Arts & Crafts Shows bring together the largest displays of silver and turquoise jewelry and American Indian arts in the U.S., with several hundred exhibitors, representing makers, dealers and traders from all the Western states. Each of the shows also features a "Demonstration Craftsmen" section, where well-known Indian artists demonstrate their crafts.

For specific annual schedules of the show, contact Tri-West Enterprises, Inc., P.O. Box 15057, Phoenix, Arizona 85018. Tel. (602) 273-1497.

MARCH

Scottsdale National Indian Arts Exhibition—The oldest and largest Indian art show in the country, the *Scottsdale National Indian Arts Exhibition* is held each year in mid-March at the Safari Hotel Convention Center in Scottsdale (4601 N. Scottsdale Road). The show, sponsored by the non-profit, volunteer *Scottsdale National Indian Arts Council Inc.*, features both traditional and contemporary arts and crafts from tribes all over North America, including Eskimos.

Last year over 3,000 items, representing the work of artists and craftsmen from 80 Indian tribes, were exhibited. Each year the Arts Council awards cash prizes amounting to several thousand dollars to young Indian student craftsmen and artists displaying their work at the show.

There is a nominal admission price to the exhibition. To confirm this year's exhibit dates, contact the Scottsdale National Indian Arts Council at Box 381, Scottsdale, Arizona 85252, or (as March approaches) the Scottsdale Chamber of Commerce. Tel. 945-8481.

MARCH–APRIL

Yaqui Easter Ceremonials—During Holy Week each year the Yaqui Indian communities of Guadalupe south of Phoenix, Old Pascua in central Tucson and New Pascua on the southwest outskirts of Tucson stage a series of religious ceremonies that outside spectators are welcome to view.

The ceremonials include the famous *Yaqui Deer Dance* and the *Burning of Judas*. The portion of the Guadalupe festival most often recommended to spectators begins at 11 a.m. on Good Friday. To reach Guadalupe from Phoenix-Scottsdale, go south to Baseline Road, proceed to 56th Street (which becomes Guadalupe Road) and turn south. The village is about 10 miles from Phoenix.

The main days at Old Pascua and New Pascua villages in Tucson are Holy Saturday before Easter, beginning at about 10 a.m., and the Saturday before Palm Sunday, beginning at sundown. The Yaqui Deer Dance is staged during the evening ceremonials.

Old Pascua is on Grant Road between Miracle Mile and the Freeway, just a few blocks north of the Tucson Hilton Inn. To reach New Pascua, take the Freeway south to Valencia Road and go west. The turn-off for the village (about a mile south of Valencia Road) is approximately three miles west of the Freeway.

APRIL

Scottsdale All Indian Pow Wow—Co-sponsored by the city of Scottsdale (Parks & Recreation Department) and the *Central Plains Indians' Club,* this major event brings together Indians from the Central Plains, Arizona and other Western states. It is held each year in April, over the first weekend following Easter.

Headquarters for the Pow Wow is the Scottsdale Stadium at Osborn Road and Civic Center Plaza. Activities and attractions include booths selling Indian arts, crafts and foods, along with Indian dance contests (with men, women and children's categories), Indian "Princess" contests, and a Saturday parade through downtown Scottsdale.

A special feature of this Pow Wow is that visitors are invited to camp out on the Pow Wow grounds during the festivities. If the stadium fills up with campers, the overflow can pitch their tents or park their vehicles at the Scottsdale Rodeo Grounds and the Boys Club Grounds. Campers are allowed to begin setting up their tents at 5 a.m. Friday morning, and may stay until 5 p.m. Sunday evening.

Among the tribes represented at last year's festivities were Navajo, Hopi, Zuni, Cheyenne, Choctaw, Apache, Pawnee, Arapaho, Fox, Shawnee, and Cherokee. Over 2,000 Indians took part in the dance contests.

Heard Museum Indian Fair—One of the best-known off-Reservation Indian events in Arizona, the *Heard Museum Indian Fair* is held in the museum auditorium at 22 E. Monte Vista Rd., Phoenix, usually over the second weekend in April. A major attraction of the Fair are demonstrations of pottery-making, rug-weaving, bead work, sand painting, basket-weaving, and other Indian arts and crafts. The items made are on sale during the Fair.

Other popular features of the Heard Museum Indian Fair include Indian dancing and food booths offering various kinds of traditional Indian dishes. Most of the Indian dancers, artists and craftsmen participating in the Fair are from Arizona tribes, but there are usually a number of better-known Zuni and Navajo craftsmen from New Mexico. A small fee is charged for admission. There is a big drawing, with prizes. Photographers are welcome.

JULY

Flagstaff All-Indian Pow Wow—This is the "granddaddy" of Arizona's off-Reservation Indian pow wows. Staged over the 4th of July holidays in alpine-cool Flagstaff, the 4-day event is attended by Indians from tribes throughout the American West, and includes ceremonial dancing, rodeos, parades, food booths and stalls selling Indian-made arts and crafts.

If you've never seen large numbers of American Indians before, this is your chance. Thousands, arriving in pick-up trucks and wagons, camp in the pine groves in and near Flagstaff during the pow wow.

Tickets for the rodeo events, ceremonial dances and Indian games may be purchased in advance from the Flagstaff Chamber of Commerce by mail or in person. Tickets may be picked up at the Chamber through June 20th. Tickets will be mailed until June 15th. After that date, mail orders must be picked up at the ticket office at the Pow Wow arena. Mail orders should be sent to the Flagstaff Chamber of Commerce, 101 W. Santa Fe Ave., Flagstaff, Arizona 86001. Tel 774-4505.

There are some 15 separate events requiring admittance tickets, ranging from $1.50 for competitive Indian dances or Indian games to $5 for the Indian

Ceremonial Dances. The latter are staged nightly at 7:30 p.m., Friday through Sunday. Children under 12 are half price.

Best idea is to contact the Chamber early and ask for a copy of their Pow Wow Program, which lists all of the events, times and prices. If you plan on staying over night, make your hotel or motel reservations weeks in advance.

Hopi Craftsmen Show—Hopi Indians demonstrate their arts and crafts at Flagstaff's famous Museum of Northern Arizona, from July 2nd through the 5th. The Museum, on Ft. Valley Road (Highway 89) three miles north of downtown Flagstaff, is itself one of the most popular attractions in northern Arizona.

Maintained by the Northern Arizona Society of Science and Art, the Museum of Northern Arizona includes a fascinating introduction to the geology, biology and anthropology of the plateaus and mountains of northern Arizona, along with an extensive selection of Indian arts and crafts on sale in its permanent Indian crafts center. During the *Hopi Craftsmen Show,* items made by the craftsmen are offered for sale.

Navajo Craftsmen Show—Another annual event at the Museum of Northern Arizona, the *Navajo Craftsmen Show* takes place during the last week in July, usually beginning on a Friday and lasting through the following Friday. This is a Navajo version of the Hopi show earlier in the month.

AUGUST

The Prescott Smoki Ceremonials—This annual event, held in mile-high Prescott on the 1st or 2nd Saturday in August, is a major attraction—even though the dancers are not Indians. Years ago, white business and civic leaders of Prescott resolved to help keep the traditions of Southwest Indian ceremonial dancing alive. They formed a group known as the *Smoki People* (pronounced "smo-kai"), carefully researched the most important Indian dances of the American Southwest and Northern Mexico, and began re-enacting the ceremonials every year.

Participants don authenticated costumes and make-up, and perform five or six of the most colorful of the Indian rituals, climaxing each annual celebration with the famous Hopi Snake Dance.

The Ceremonials are staged at the Yavapai County Fairgrounds, beginning at sundown, Saturday night. There is only one performance. All seating is reserved, and tickets are available only from the *Smoki People* organization. To order tickets in advance, write to: Smoki People, P.O. Box 123, Prescott, Arizona 86301.

OCTOBER

Holbrook All-Indian Rodeo—Holbrook, on Highway 66 near the southern boundary of Navajo Land, is on the circuit of the *All-Indian Rodeo Cowboy*

Association, which sponsors many of the Indian cowboy rodeos in Arizona. The All-Indian rodeo season starts in April, currently at Window Rock on the Navajo Reservation, and ends in October, with the finals scheduled for Holbrook.

At this writing, the All-Indian Rodeo Cowboy Association, with over 1,000 members, stages 26 rodeos a year. The goal is 35 rodeos a year, with the finals held in a major city such as Phoenix. Dates of the Holbrook All-Indian rodeo vary, but are now set for the second or third weekend in October. To confirm, check with the Holbrook Chamber of Commerce (324 Navajo Blvd., Holbrook, Arizona 86025. Tel. 524-6558) in August or September.

Again, the date (month as well as day) of the Holbrook rodeo is subject to change in accordance with the annual schedule of the Indian Rodeo Association.

NOVEMBER–DECEMBER

The Heard Museum Guild Annual Indian Arts & Crafts Exhibit—This is the second of the Indian events sponsored by the Heard Museum Guild each year. Held over a 10-day period in late November and early December, the Exhibit features the works of Indian artists and craftsmen from all over North America, including Canada and Alaska.

The exhibit includes 12 categories of arts and crafts, the largest of which are usually paintings, jewelry and pottery. The exhibit is a "judge show," with winning craftsmen and artists in each of the 12 categories receiving cash awards amounting to several thousand dollars.

Those interested in receiving announcements about the show are invited to send their name and address to the Heard Museum, 22 E. Monte Vista Road, Phoenix, Arizona 85004.

Add Copy

FEBRUARY

O'odham Tash Casa Grande Indian Pow Wow—Held over the second weekend in February (Washington's Birthday weekend), this popular annual event includes parades, barbecues, Indian ceremonial dances, music by Indian bands, Indian arts and crafts sales and demonstrations, and rodeos. Main action begins Saturday morning and continues on through Monday evening. Casa Grande is adjacent to I-10 about midway between Phoenix and Tucson. For additional details, contact the Casa Grande Chamber of Commerce, 201 E. 4th St., Casa Grande, Arizona 85222. Tel. 836-2125.